LUCI
O'SULL

Little Black Book of
Great Places to Stay
2007

IRELAND

Enchanting Houses, Inns
Castles, Hotels and Spas

TSAR PRESS

This book is published by

TSAR PRESS

Post Office Box No. 9647
Glenageary, Co. Dublin.

www.lucindaosullivan.com
www.wheretostayinireland.com

Written and collated by Lucinda O'Sullivan
Publishing Editor Brendan O'Sullivan

Regional Editor Margaret Browne
Maps and Mapping Joe Morris
Technical Support Ian O'Sullivan
Cover Ian O'Sullivan
Layout Susan Waine, Ashfield Press

Lucinda O'Sullivan has asserted her right to be identified
as author of this book

ISBN-10 0-9547256-2-X
ISBN-13 978-0-9547256-2-4
EAN 9780954725624

Printed in Ireland by Betaprint Limited

A word from Lucinda

In 2004 when my first Little Black Book of Great Places to Stay was published it was an instant success. People had been writing and emailing, knowing that in my role as Restaurant Critic of the Sunday Independent I was travelling the country and, as well as eating, I also had to find a bed for the night! This gave me an unparrelled opportunity each week to experience the good, the bad, and the ugly, of tourist accommodation in Ireland. It is a subject always close to my heart, as I started out my career in the Tourism Industry more years ago than I care to remember, as they say. But, my goodness, how things have changed over the intervening years. Even since 2004 there have been leaps and bounds – its like the change in the aero industry from piston powered engines to jet propelled!

What we have seen here is the demise of the ordinary B & B with nylon sheets, skinny breakfasts, watery smiles and give me the money attitudes. People have a much better standard of living nowadays - interiors and food are a passion – and nobody will tolerate that type of miserable "welcome" anymore. The sad thing is that some of these B & B owners haven't yet seen the wood for the trees and are bleating and wondering where their business is gone. What has taken over are lavish Guesthouses with all the facilities and comforts of home. There are cracking designer hotels and the country is now awash with gorgeous Spas. Traditional family hotels have also been progressing with the times, embarking on stunning makeovers.

I have stayed in countless houses and hotels and I have learned that the most expensive lauded or grand establishment is not necessarily the greatest or the most enjoyable place to stay for often they can be carried away with their own importance, be chilly, uncaring and offhand.

The Castles, Inns, Country and City Houses, Spas and special Hotels included in my Little Black Book for 2007 are rich in their thinking and attitude towards the guest and the tourists. Some are lavish and luxurious, some are simple and sincere, some are creative and humorous, but here you can expect at all different levels, the finest of what Ireland has to offer by way of hospitality, friendship, helfulness and value for money in each category.

Don't forget to use my website www.lucindaosullivan.com through which you can contact me, share your experiences, and let me know if you have any wonderful discoveries.

Get out there and enjoy.

Lucinda

Ireland

reland, perceived as the Emerald Isle, Land of the Shamrock, the Leprechaun, the Blarney Stone, Thatched and White Washed Cottages, and the attitude of "as God made time he made plenty of it" has changed dramatically in recent years. It is now a thriving progressive country holding its head high as a member of the European Union but City traffic is bumper to bumper from early morning as workers head for their places of employment to keep the wheels of progress turning. However, underneath all the hustle and bustle, people haven't changed all that much. They still like to meet and talk, share a story, have a laugh and generally enjoy life.

Sport is a major interest here. Our bloodstock industry, both racing and show jumping is respected world-wide. Irish golf courses are a match for any in the World and our golfers, of the standing of Padraig Harrington, Darren Clarke, Paul McGinley, regularly contest major competitions internationally. Rugby and soccer both have a solid following but the major football game is Gaelic football with interest reaching its climax at the end of September when the all Ireland Final between the two leading Counties is played. For visitors possibly the most fascinating sport is traditional hurling, which is probably the fastest field game in the world, requiring speed, fitness, physical strength, great skill and application.

The open countryside, from the pleasant valleys and rounded mountains of the East to the rugged features of the West, provide ample scope and pleasant diversity of scenery for the walker or cyclist. For the motorist there are limitless places of interest from ancient ruins, fine buildings and museums, breathtaking scenery and even a Fairy Tree on the Comeragh drive near Dungarvan. The gourmet is well catered for as each and every county provides some excellent Restaurants to please even the most demanding palate.

Most pubs and bars provide good value lunches during the day and, in the evenings, many of them have traditional musicians and singers and, as we say in Ireland, the craic.

Most of all, apart from the sport, scenery, food, drink, craic, music the main attraction must be the people themselves, generally warm friendly and welcoming.

Ireland – you won't be disappointed.

EXPLANATION OF SYMBOLS

The symbols are a guide to facilities rather that a positive statement, and may change, so check important points when booking.

Working Farm

Children welcome, no age limits, but cots, high chairs etc are not necessarily available.

Credit Cards accepted – generally Visa/MC

T.V. in bedrooms

Swimming pool on premises

P   Parking

Wine License – Hotels have full licenses

Disabled Facilities – check level with establishment.

Non-Smoking House

Pets welcome but may have to sleep in outbuilding or car. Check.

Pets accommodated in house.

Bikes on loan or for hire.

Tennis Court on premises

H   Helipad

NET   Internet access

Spa   Spa

9h   9 Hole Golf Course on Site

18h   18 Hole Golf Course on Site

Contents

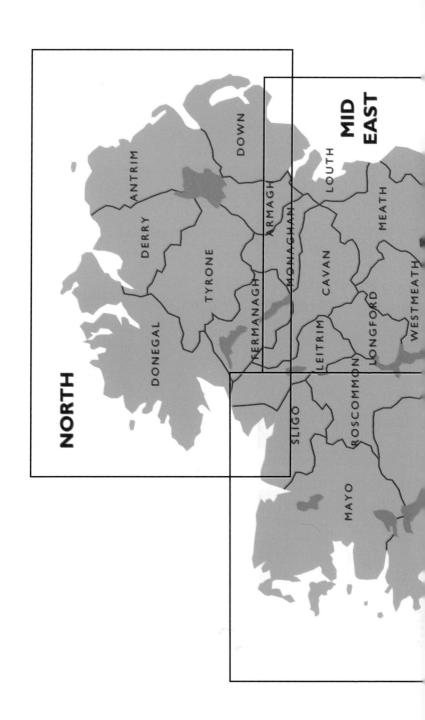

NORTH

MID EAST

ANTRIM
DOWN
DERRY
ARMAGH
LOUTH
TYRONE
MONAGHAN
MEATH
DONEGAL
FERMANAGH
CAVAN
LEITRIM
LONGFORD
WESTMEATH
SLIGO
ROSCOMMON
MAYO

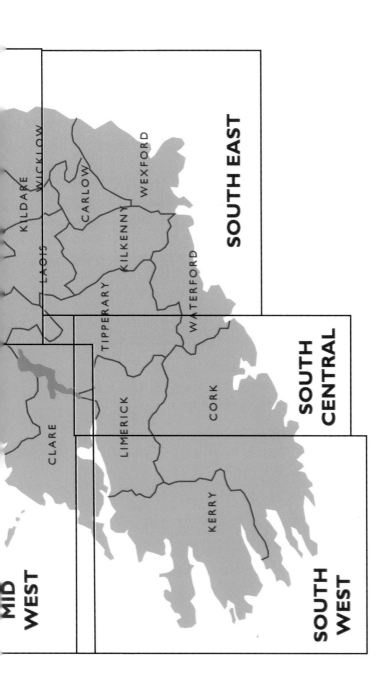

MID WEST

SOUTH EAST

SOUTH CENTRAL

SOUTH WEST

KILDARE

WICKLOW

LAOIS

CARLOW

WEXFORD

KILKENNY

TIPPERARY

WATERFORD

CLARE

LIMERICK

CORK

KERRY

North

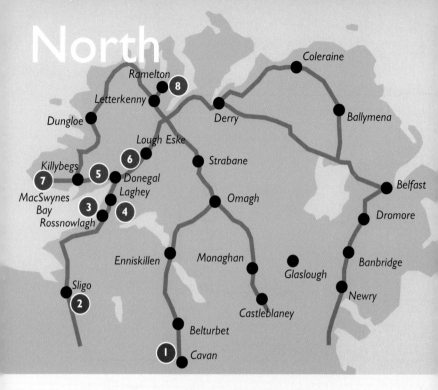

1. Cavan Crystal Hotel
2. Kingsfort Country House
3. The Sandhouse Hotel & Marine Spa
4. Coxtown Manor
5. Donegal Manor
6. Harvey's Point Country Hotel
7. CastleMurray House Hotel
8. Frewin

1. The Merrion Hotel
2. Conrad Hotel Dublin
3. Dylan Boutique Hotel
4. Hotel Isaacs
5. Aberdeen Lodge
6. Drummond Mews
7. Redbank House & Restaurant
8. Dunboyne Castle
9. Carton House
10. Tankardstown House
11. Cavan Crystal Hotel
12. Shamrock Lodge
13. The County Arms

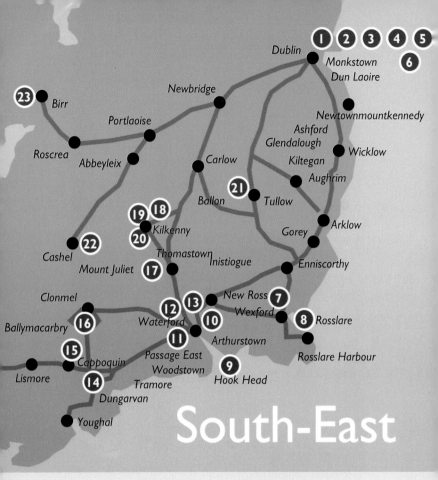

South-East

1. The Merrion Hotel
2. Conrad Hotel Dublin
3. Dylan Boutique Hotel
4. Aberdeen Lodge
5. Hotel Isaacs
6. Drummond Mews
7. White's Hotel & Spa
8. Kelly's Resort Hotel & Spa
9. Aldridge Lodge
10. Glendine Country House
11. Foxmount Country House
12. Waterford Castle
13. Athenaeum House Hotel
14. Cairbre House
15. Richmond House
16. Glasha Country House
17. Mount Juliet Conrad
18. Lacken House
19. Kilkenny Hibernian Hotel
20. Langton's Hotel
21. Ballyderrin House & Cookery School
22. Bailey's Of Cashel
23. The County Arms

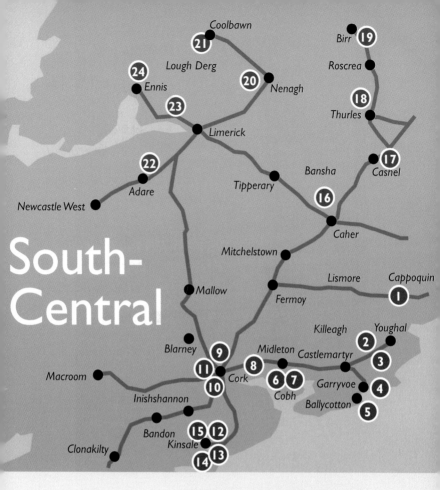

South-Central

1. Richmond House
2. Ballymakeigh Country House
3. Inchiquin House
4. Garryvoe Hotel
5. Bayview Hotel
6. Sheraton Fota Island Resort
7. Knockeven Country House
8. Radisson SAS Cork
9. Hotel Isaac's Cork
10. Hayfield Manor
11. Crawford House
12. Blue Haven Hotel
13. Friar's Lodge
14. Old Bank House
15. Shearwater
16. Bansha Castle
17. Bailey's Hotel
18. Inch House
19. The County Arms
20. Ashley Park House
21. Coolbawn Quay Lakeshore Spa
22. Dunraven Arms
23. Bunratty Manor
24. Old Ground Hotel

South-West

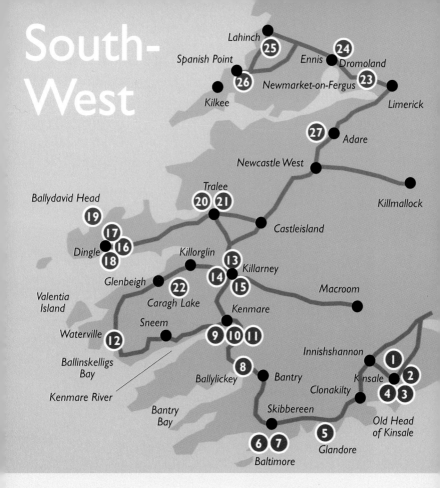

1. Blue Haven Hotel
2. Friar's Lodge
3. The Old Bank House
4. Shearwater
5. Kilfinnan Farmhouse
6. Baltimore Harbour Hotel
7. Baltimore Bay Guesthouse
8. Seaview House Hotel
9. Muxnaw Lodge
10. Brook Lane Hotel
11. Virginia's Guest House
12. Butler Arms Hotel
13. Aghadoe Heights Hotel & Spa
14. Cahernane House Hotel
15. Muckross Park Hotel & Spa
16. Bambury's Guest House
17. Heaton's Guesthouse
18. Castlewood House
19. Gorman's Clifftop House & Restaurant
20. Manor West Hotel
21. Meadowlands Hotel
22. Carrig House
23. Bunratty Manor
24. Old Ground Hotel
25. Vaughan Lodge
26. Admiralty Lodge
27. Dunraven Arms

Mid-West

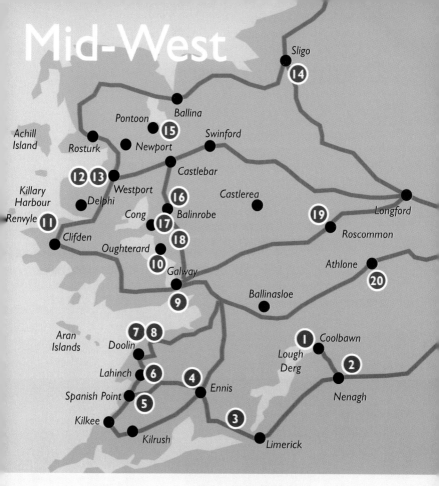

1	Coolbawn Quay Lakeshore Spa	12	Ardmore House Hotel
2	Ashley Park House	13	Knockranny House Hotel
3	Bunratty Manor	14	Kingsfort Country House
4	Old Ground Hotel	15	Pontoon Bridge Hotel
5	Admiralty Lodge	16	JJ Gannon' Hotel
6	Vaughan Lodge	17	Ashford Castle
7	Ballyvara House	18	Ballywarren Country House
8	Ballinalacken Castle	19	Gleeson's Townhouse
9	Galway Radisson SAS Hotel	20	Shamrock Lodge
10	Ross Lake House Hotel		
11	Renvyle House Hotel		

County Carlow

Carlow is a low-rise busy midlands Town, on the River Barrow, and was an Anglo Norman stronghold at the edge of a very Gaelic county. Its present calm and serene atmosphere belies its turbulent past. At its heart is a beautiful classical Courthouse with the portico modelled on the Parthenon. Also worth seeing in Carlow is the controversial Regency Gothic Cathedral designed by Pugin. For those interested in Irish brew the Celtic Brewing Company, beside the Railway Station, is worth a tour. The beers brewed there are based on traditional Celtic recipes including a wheat beer, red ale and stout. Carlow has become a commuter town from Dublin and is developing rapidly, hence a plethora of new boutiques, restaurants, bars and cafes. Lennons and La Strada on Tullow Street are good buzzy spots with decent food. Teach Dolmen, also in Tullow Street, has impromptu traditional Irish music

sessions. Two miles east of town on the R726 is Browneshill Dolmen, possibly the largest Neolithic stone formation in Europe dating from 2500 BC. Seven miles south of Carlow on the N 9 is Leighlinbridge, the birthplace of Cardinal Cullen. Altamont Gardens near Tullow and Ballon are beautiful and attract many visitors. Borris, St. Mullins and the South Leinster Way are very popular with walkers and cyclists and are a great weekend destination. Carlow is mainly a farming county, which accounts for its easy going and generous atmosphere.

"You'll never plough a field by turning it over in your mind"
(Irish Proverb)

Ballyderrin House

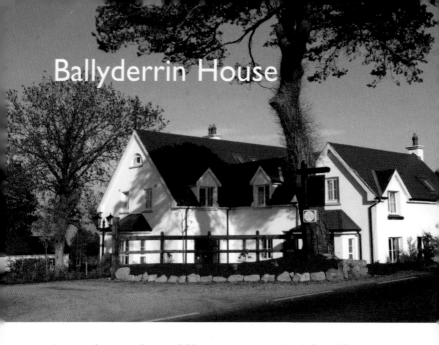

My happiest days as child were spent at my Aunt's farm, The Grange, in Tullow. Hours were spent running up and down the avenue under dark overhanging trees, the best swing in the world was a branch of a big horse chestnut tree on the lawn, and days were spent "driving" a rusty old tractor skeleton. Tullow is a pretty town with a statue in the square erected to Fr. John Murphy who was "brutally put to death by the British". Uncle Tom took a visiting brother in law from England into town for a pint and, when the poor man saw the inscription on the statue, he thought he would never get back to the safety of Birmingham!

BALLYDERRIN HOUSE

Pamela and John Holligan's comfortable Ballyderrin House is on two acres of gardens surrounded by glorious countryside and woodland, against a backdrop of the Wicklow Mountains. Ballyderrin however is not just a place to rest one's weary head, for you are going to be under the care of a very fine cook. Pamela spent fifteen years in London working in top foodie establishments and is also Ballymaloe trained, so you are assured of beautifully prepared and presented food – organic where possible.

Having subsequently taught in Ballymaloe, Pamela set up her excellent Ballyderrin Cookery

School. The School offers day, weekend and evening courses, which are held in fully equipped purpose built classrooms, under the tuition of highly skilled experts. So, you can combine a holiday, or a break, with acquiring knowledge. Pamela's cookery classes are fun too – I loved the idea of her BBQ evenings where, for a very reasonable charge, hubbie, partner or friends can come and join in when the food is cooked and make an evening out of the event. Aga Cookery weekends are very popular too, a great way to make new friends and enjoy the food together that you have cooked. Don't forget to visit their Café and Country Store and stock up with delicious jams, chutneys, breads, organic spices, herbs and wines

   Ballyderrin is ideally located, just ten minutes walk from the centre of the town, and from Mount Wolseley's Championship golf course if you fancy swinging a club. It is also an ideal fishing location along the River Slaney and they have facilities for pets.

   I feel a trip to Tullow coming on …

Owners:	Pamela and John Holligan	
Address:	Shillelagh Road,	
	Tullow,	
	Co. Carlow.	
Tel	059 9152742	
No. Of Rooms	6	
Price		
Double/Twin	€70 -€80	
Single	€50 -€55	
Family	€80 + 20% for extra person. €5 child under 5.	
Dinner	Yes (must be booked in advance)	
Open	All Year – Closed 24th, 25th, 26th December.	
Credit Cards	All Major Cards	
Directions	From Tullow take the R725 towards Shillelagh	
	Out of town _ mile on left.	
Email	ballyderrinhouse@eircom.net	
Web	www.lucindaosullivan.com/ballyderrin	

County Cavan

County Cavan, for years rather neglected as a holiday and leisure area, is becoming more popular as people discover what the county has to offer. A factor in this has been the opening of the Shannon-Erne waterway linking streams, rivers and lakes through almost forty miles of beautiful unspoiled countryside and making an attractive destination for pleasure boat users. The county is also a popular venue for anglers from both home and abroad.

Cavan town is the ideal centre for exploring the many lakes and rivers of the county. Quiet and friendly, the town's many shops provide all the goodies any tourist might require. The Lough Oughter area in the north of the county is a major focus of scenic interest. Belturbet on the River Erne is a popular angling and boating centre with a marina and

cruiser centre and boats available for rental. Killeshandra is a good place if your interest is in traditional music and, eleven miles south of Cavan town, is Ballyjamesduff, the home of the County Cavan Museum with an impressive collection which covers all aspects of the county's history. The town was made famous by the beautiful Percy French song – "Come Back Paddy Reilly to Ballyjamesduff". The county is also unique in that its Gaelic football team won the All Ireland Title in 1947, the only time it was ever played outside of Ireland. It was played that year in the Polo Grounds in New York, in commeration of the 100th anniversary of the Great Famine.

"All you need to be a fisherman is patience and a worm"
(Herb Shriner)

Cavan Crystal Hotel

If you want a destination where you can dine well, be pampered in a Health and Beauty Clinic, and shop 'til you drop, well it has to be the Cavan Crystal Hotel. It is a Hotel with a difference – funky bright beautiful – fabulous contemporary design showcased in a Hotel that has the Cavan Crystal Showrooms under the one roof for it is under the same ownership.

Cavan is a beautiful county, full of romantic lakes and forests, plenty of golf courses, but it really needed a special hotel and this gap has now been filled. The enormously high Atrium, filled with light and magnificent chandeliers, is stunning and you realize immediately this place has been done with style.

There are 85 gorgeous bedrooms fitted out to very high specifications with lovely crisp bedlinen, beautiful covers and throws, fluffy bathrobes, remote control television, bottled water, ironing facilities, so there is everything you could possibly want. If you really want to push out the boat there is always the Presidential Suite. Need a lift after the journey? Book yourself into the Utopia Health & Beauty Clinic for an Express Facial or maybe a Hydro-Active Mineral Salt Scrub. There is also the Azuma Hair Salon.

Cavan Crystal are very keen on sourcing local producers – indeed they host an Annual Awards for the best Irish small producers - so you can be sure what you are eating is good. Their Opus One Restaurant is sleek and bright and the food is cracking. Think maybe of kicking off with foie gras terrine,

mango jelly, crisp ginger bread and a sharp raspberry reduction or baked goats cheese and pumpkin seed tartlet, white onion mousseline and beetroot ice. Follow up maybe with panfried fillet of seabass and scallop with baby fennel, millefeuille of tomato and fennel icecream. They also do delicious roasted scallops on Asian vegetables with a fig and loganberry dressing. Wow.

You will certainly enjoy your visit to the Lake County if you make the Cavan Crystal Hotel your destination.

Owners	Siobhan Smyth, General Manager.
Address	Dublin Road, Cavan.
Tel:	049 4360600
No of Rooms	85
Price	
Double/twin	From €170
Single	From €110
Family	From €170
Dinner	Yes - Restaurant
Open	All year save Christmas Day
Credit Cards	Yes
Directions	Located on the Dublin Road on the outskirts of Cavan Town, just off the N3. A location map can be downloaded from their website.
Email	info@cavancrystalhotel.com
Web	www.lucindaosullivan.com/cavancrystalhotel

NET Spa H P

County Clare

County Clare is bordered by Galway to the north – the Atlantic to the west and the River Shannon on the east and south. Renowned as a stronghold of traditional music, it also offers many other attractions to the visitor. The Burren is a stark expanse of moonlike grey limestone and shale which is home to the most extraordinary flora and fauna and is a must visit. Kilkee is a seaside resort popular with families and scuba divers and has plenty of restaurants and pubs. Lahinch with its fabulous broad beach attracts surfers and boasts a

magnificent golf course. The Cliffs of Moher attract a number of visitors as does the town of Doolin, four miles from the Cliffs. Doolin is for many the music centre of the west and you are sure to find some kind of merriment in one of the town's pubs (O'Connor's, McCann's and McDermott's). If you are unmarried and visit Lisdoonvarna in the month of September you may well find yourself "Spoken For" before you leave, for the town is famous for its month long Matchmaking Festival which comes after the Harvest has been saved.

Wedlock – "the deep, deep peace of the double bed after the hurly burly of the chaise longue"
(Mrs. Patrick Campbell)

Admiralty Lodge

As a Canadian friend said to me, the remote rugged beauty of Clare is the Real Ireland, its what visitors want to see, and what many of us want to escape to. Out to the very west of County Clare is Spanish Point, with its enormous white crested waves, azure blue seas, crystal clear blue skies, its absolutely unspoilt magnificence is virtually unmatched. Having been to the Burren and the Cliffs of Moher, we were cruising down the coast road when we spotted a very new and interesting looking white building with Irish and American flags flying.

Pat O'Malley's luxury 4 Star Country House is the best thing to have happened in centuries in County Clare. First thing I noticed was the large purple modern chaise longue in the hall. Then I looked into a beautiful anti-room, and on to the even more magnificent diningroom with grand piano in front of French Doors to the garden. I think this is probably the most beautiful diningroom in the country. The high, barrel shaped, white panelled ceiling holds three crystal chandeliers, which shimmer in the large over mantels at each end of the room. One wall is similarly panelled half way up and then dressed with sophisticated floral fabric whilst the other is red brick.

Well, you can't eat the décor, I can hear you say, but the food too is divine and not overpriced for its elegant simplicity and surroundings. This is a serious kitchen producing contemporary classical cuisine. Dinner might include Seared Scallops with an avocado mousse or a simply described Quail and new potato salad belying not so simple Ballotine of breast meat, drizzled with a fine frothy reduction, and the quail's leg perched on a baby new potato with a balsamic reduction. You might follow this up with perfectly pink trefoiled rump of lamb on sweet potato with caramelised sweetbreads – and you'll die for the desserts.

Bedrooms are spacious, beautifully furnished, with king-size four-poster beds, Armoires, Chinoiserie wallpaper, and flat screen LCD televisions. I could

hide in one of those rooms for a week and then sneak out to a local Seisun for the craic. Marbled bathrooms have power showers designed to either kill the hangover or administer an in-shower exfoliation.

Admiralty Lodge is perfect for golfers, for lovers, for foodies, take the helicopter or the batmobile and go now.

Owner:	Pat & Aoife O'Malley
Address:	Spanish Point, Miltown Malbay, Co. Clare.
Tel	065 7085007
No.of Rooms	12
Prices	
Double/Twin	From €160 - €220
Single	From €100 - €150
Dinner	Yes – Piano Room Diningroom
Open	March - December
Credit Cards	Yes
Directions	From Ennis (Clare's main Town) take the Lahinch/Milltown
Malbay	Road. In Milltown take the Spanish Point Road, follow signposts to Admiralty Lodge.
Email:	info@admiralty.ie
Web:	www.lucindaosullivan.com/admiralty

Ballinalacken Castle Country House Hotel

Even the name sounds romantic – you just couldn't invent it. It smacks of history and romance – crashing waves, lusty thighs, flowing hair - young men and beautiful girls out on the wild stormy cliffs of Clare. What a field day novelist Daphne du Maurier could have had down here writing about her pirates a la Frenchman's Creek.

The historic Ballinalacken House is located in one of the most stunning situations on the western seaboard with spectacular views of the Aran Islands, the Cliffs of Moher, just ten minutes away, and Galway Bay. The house was built by Lord O'Brien in 1840 standing in the shadow of the ruins of the O'Brien Clan's 15th c Ballinalacken Castle. It was his family home and remained as such for 99 years until, in 1939, it was bought by the present family. The beautiful rooms have been restored to their original grandeur, antiques, lovely cornice work, light fittings, and splendid marble mantelpieces on which to rest your glass of port. All of the bedrooms are lovely. Some have four poster beds for that really romantic visit and there are four superior rooms and two beautiful suites.

If you have been out playing golf all day, or touring, or visiting the Burren – for which Ballinalacken could not be better placed – you want to be able to dump the car when you get back and crash out with really good food and wines. They have a cute little rustic "pub" bar where you can have

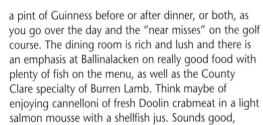

a pint of Guinness before or after dinner, or both, as you go over the day and the "near misses" on the golf course. The dining room is rich and lush and there is an emphasis at Ballinalacken on really good food with plenty of fish on the menu, as well as the County Clare specialty of Burren Lamb. Think maybe of enjoying cannelloni of fresh Doolin crabmeat in a light salmon mousse with a shellfish jus. Sounds good, doesn't it? It gets better. At Ballinalacken pan seared fillets of John Dory are served French style with a barigole of artichokes and port whilst supreme of Barbary duck is served on a celeriac puree complemented by Guinness and Fresh honey sauce – now that's a talking point.

Grab your cailin by the waist and go...it might change your life.

Owner	Denis O'Callaghan
Address	Coast Road, Doolin, Co. Clare.
Tel:	065 7074025
No of Rooms	12
Price	
Double/twin	€140 (DBB packages available – April and October specials at €99)
Dinner	Yes - restaurant
Open	Early April – End October
Credit Cards	Yes
Directions	Take R476 north of Doolin. 2 miles at junction R476 + R477 is hotel. From Lisdoonvarna take R477 coast road – 3 miles from town.
Email	ballinalackencastle@eircom.net
Web	www.lucindaosullivan.com/ballinalackencastle

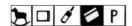

Ballyvara House

Doolin is a pretty and popular village, in a dramatic setting, just four miles north of the Cliffs of Moher, close to the Burren, and ten minutes from Lahinch if you are a golfer! Also a take off point for the Aran Islands, it makes an ideal place in which to base oneself. Visit the sights during the day and enjoy the pubs and seisiuns at night. You want somewhere nice to stay that is where Ballyvara House comes into play.

Ballyvara was once a charming farm cottage which John Flanagan inherited and which he turned into an approved B & B. However, John, a joiner and builder, took the idea much further and, retaining the stone and timber of the old cottage, has transformed the place into the spanking new Guest House it is today. Bedrooms are large and all have queen size beds, spa or Jacuzzi baths, some even have balconies with stunning views. There are a couple of suites complete with a large lounge with big T.V, mini-bar, mini plasma flat screen T.V. and safes if you don't want to carry around your valuables while sightseeing.

Located on 20 acres, there is a pretty courtyard garden but also plenty of room to romp around and children will love to go out and visit the donkey duo, Shetland and Welsh ponies, and dogs, as well as enjoy the new Play Area. They have also added a multi purpose astro turf playing court. Ballyvara is a fun place with a little residents' bar where you can meet other visitors, have a drink and a bit of craic, and not worry about having to drive

home. Excellent reasonably priced food is available in their new adjoining Tir Gaw Gan House Hotel. It might be crab claws; Burren smoked salmon roulade. Follow up then with the fish dish of the evening or Barbary duck breast or steak. They always do a vegetarian dish and they have an extensive wine list. Breakfasts are brilliant – you can have the Full Irish or the Empty Irish and that, in case you didn't know, is eggs, bacon and tomato, without the sausage, pudding and beans! They also do delicious omelettes and luscious pancakes with syrup… If you so desire, instead of making a breakfast deadline…you can even have your breakfast in bed…most unusual for a Guest House.

John and Becky are welcoming hosts – you will be glad you discovered Ballyvara – I was.

Owners:	John Flanagan
Address:	Ballyvara, Doolin, Co. Clare.
Tel	065 7074467
No. Of Rooms	11
Price	Double/Twin €70/€200
Dinner	Yes – in next door hotel under same ownership.
Open	All Year – Closed 22-28 December
Credit Cards	Visa MC Amex Laser
Directions	Once in Doolin village - from Roadford take the first Left after Cullinan's Restaurant (on right); Ballyvara is half mile up hill on left.
Email:	info@ballyvara.ie
Web:	www.lucindaosullivan.com/ballyvarahouse

BUNRATTY

Bunratty is one of those places in Ireland that brings shamrocks to your eyes! But seriously folks, the whole Bunratty experience is great fun, from the possibility of being the one chosen to be "thrown in the dungeon" at the Mediaeval Banquet in the Castle, to a visit to Durty Nelly's Pub. Bunratty Castle is well worth a visit even if you don't do the banquet for it is perfectly restored and houses a large collection of historic furniture, paintings and tapestries. In the grounds of the castle too is the Bunratty Folk Park which is a reconstruction of a 19th century Irish village.

BUNRATTY MANOR

You won't be thrown in the dungeon at Bunratty Manor. Quite the contrary, for you will be welcomed with open arms by the Squire and his good lady, Noel and Fiona Wallace, and fed and watered to your heart's content.

Bunratty Manor is a comfortable small modern family hotel offering personalised service, which can make all the difference to one's stay. The bedrooms are extremely comfortable and spacious with all mod cons and decent orthopaedic beds, crisp cotton and linens. There is multi channel TV, tea and coffee making facilites and pretty well anything one would want – and if there isn't Noel will do his best to get it for you – he is that sort of chap – friendly and helpful.

The Manor Room Restaurant is extremely popular in its own right so make sure you book in advance when making your accommodation reservation. Their fish is delivered three times weekly from the Atlantic harbour in beautiful Kenmare Bay. They believe in using local produce and their meats and vegetables come from the lush green pastures that abound in south west Ireland. They also have a cracking wine list to suit all pockets.

Bunratty Manor is a great place to stay, close to Limerick and to Shannon Airport, and there is plenty to do and see.

Slainte

Owners	Noel & Fiona Wallace
Address	Bunratty, Co. Clare.
Tel:	061 707984
No of Rooms	23
Price	
Double/twin	€150
Single	€105
Family	€180
Dinner	Yes - Restaurant
Open	All Year
Credit Cards	Yes
Directions	N18 from Limerick. Exit to Bunratty. 1st property on right on entering the village.
Email	bunrattymanor@eircom.net
Web	www.lucindaosullivan.com/bunrattymanor

Old Ground Hotel

The Gardening Editor of the up market American magazine, Traditional Home, was visiting Ireland last year and what, of course, would be a gardens tour of Ireland if it did not incorporate the Burren. We then worked our way further down through County Clare and found ourselves in Ennis. "Let's go to the Old Ground." I said. She was flying out of Shannon next day. Well, was I ever in for a surprise. I had been there a few years earlier and I hardly recognized the place. It was, and is, just amazingly beautiful now - like a thoroughbred gorgeous Country House with all the modern conveniences of a Hotel.

The Old Ground was a former manor house built in the 18th century as a private residence. In 1946 with the advent of transatlantic flights into Shannon Airport an extension was built onto the house. Meals were served throughout the night for TWA and Pan Am crews. Next door was the Town Hall, which incorporated a jail and this became part of the Old Ground Hotel.

The Old Ground was bought by Allen Flynn of the Flynn Hotel Group and, oh boy, has it ever had a makeover. It is hard to know where to start for the public areas, drawingrooms, resident's library, bars are all beautifully draped and furnished. There is a magnificent private contemporary art collection throughout and details like this make such a difference. The bedrooms are beautifully equipped with crisp white linen. the softest squishy

duvets and pillows, all mod cons, and cracking bathrooms. Rooms with air-conditioning, seating areas, sound systems and Wireless Internet access are also available. There are plenty of places to eat. We loved their Town Hall Bistro with its stone walls, cool décor, where we had sesame crusted seabass with dill scented couscous which came with an unusual lime and chardonnay butter, and roast rack of Clare lamb with a balsamic and port reduction. You can pop in here all day and have morning coffee and scones or afternoon tea. There is also the more formal red and gold themed O'Brien Room where the food is superb.

"I'm going to come back here next year" my guest said. "The whole place just has a magical feel." I felt really good showing off such a beautiful establishment.

Owners	Mary Gleeson (General Manager)
Address	O'Connell Street, Ennis, Co. Clare.
Tel:	065 6828127
No of Rooms	110
Price	
Double/twin	€110-€180
Single	€85 - €115
Family	€150 - €200
Dinner	Yes – Restaurant, Bistro and Bar Food
Open	All year Save Christmas Day
Credit Cards	Yes
Directions	From Limerick, follow signs for Galway/Shannon Airport N18
Email	reservations@oldgroundhotel.ie
Web	www.lucindaosullivan.com/flynnhotels

Vaughan Lodge

There are certain counties that are always on the visitor's list when they come to Ireland and Clare is one of them. It is one of the most "away from it all" places you could possibly be in - the Real Ireland of both yesterday and today. It remains untouched and splendiferous and, in so many ways, is quite heartbreakingly beautiful and nostalgic. They come to visit the amazing Cliffs of Moher; to play golf and feel the breeze of the Atlantic; to visit the natural phenomenon that is the Burren.

You can take in all that County Clare has to offer and indulge in absolutely delicious food as well. My interest in Vaughan Lodge was sparked when I heard that the superb French Chef Philippe Farineau had moved from his former base in Cork to this spanking new Boutique Hotel in Lahinch. I knew then that young couple Michael and Maria Vaughan were serious and professional in their enterprise. They say that good hoteliers aren't made they are bred and that can certainly be said of Michael Vaughan who is fourth generation of his family of hoteliers but who has grasped with vigour and enthusiasm what is required by today's discerning guest and, by gosh, Michael and Maria are providing it.

Bedrooms are done in contemporary style with state of the art facilities so what you really have here is country house ambience with all of the comforts and facilities of a sleek state of the art hotel. Have a cocktail or a "ball of malt" in the evenings in the cocktail club lounge and replay your golf round before dinner. That brings me back to Phillippe. The Vaughan's modestly suggest in their promotional brochure that you book dinner one

evening in the restaurant during your stay. I would respectfully suggest that you book dinner in their restaurant every evening of your stay ... you will not find better in Lahinch. Think maybe of Variation Sur La Langoustine de Galway – a fresh prawn four way tasting – Crème Brulee – Risotto – Consommé – Wonton- followed up maybe by Lobster on butternut squash, baby spinach and lobster froth ... or gorgeous Burren Lamb with Boulangere potato ... and you will get a complementary half bottle of House Champagne and chocolates if you mention the *Little Black Book* on making your booking...

Vaughan Lodge is a serious addition to County Clare gourmet golfer's repertoire.

Owners	Michael Vaughan
Address	Vaughan Lodge, Ennistymon Road, Lahinch, Co. Clare.
Tel:	065 7081111
No of Rooms	22
Price	
Double/twin	€160 - €250
Single	€95 - €155
Dinner	Yes - Restaurant
Open	Mid March – 31st October
Credit Cards	Yes
Directions	Situated on the eastern side of the village of Lahinch on the N67 Just inside the 50 KMP sign.
Email	info@vaughanlodge.ie
Web	www.lucindaosullivan.com/vaughanlodge

County Cork

Known as the Rebel County, for past deeds and the fact that Michael Collins was a native, Cork is the largest county in Ireland. An area of lush fertile farming land, and of fabulously indented coastline, it is also site of Ireland's second City. On the eastern side of the county there is the impressive little fishing port of Ballycotton. Close by is Shanagarry Pottery which is well worth a visit. Further along the coast is the historic town of Cobh, the harbour from which thousands of Irish emigrants departed for the U.S. and Australia, and was the last port of call of the ill fated Titanic. Close by Cobh is Fota Wildlife Park and, not far away, is a spot close to the heart of most Irish men – Midleton – the home of Jameson's Irish whiskey. Travel further west and visit Blarney Castle where you can kiss the famed Blarney Stone, said to endow one with the gift of the gab. Kinsale with its impressive Forts, narrow streets, and yachting marina is a picturesque town, and known as the gourmet capital of Ireland. Moving on west through Clonakilty you come to Rosscarbery, with its lovely Continental type village square, but swing left off the main road and wend your way to magnificent Glandore. Stop, take a seat by the wall, overlooking the water and have lunch. Take it easy and enjoy the peace. Further West is the nautically inclined very popular Baltimore. Travel on to Bantry Town which overlooks the famous bay of the same name and you can visit magnificent Bantry House, home of many art treasures. Move on then to the lushness and splendour of Ballylicky and Glengarriff, the last stop before entering the Kingdom of Kerry. And what about Cork City you might ask, for we Dubliners know that Cork is the "real" capital of Ireland. It is a major port on the estuary of the River Lee and this both lively and relaxed City is one of the most pleasurable urban areas in Ireland and is the south's self proclaimed cultural capital. This fantastic county with its rich pastoral land and its rugged coastline of beautiful bays and inlets has many places of historic and cultural interest and the natives are very friendly.

"Culture is roughly anything we do and monkeys don't"

(Lord Raglan)

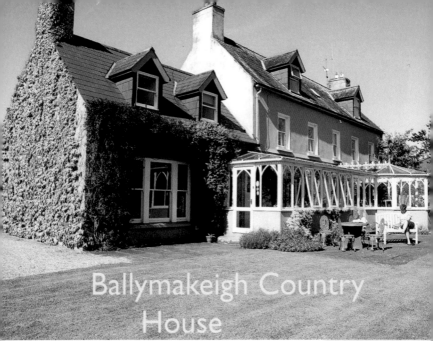

Ballymakeigh Country House

As if on cue, 200 glorious Friesian cows trundled from the fields, in what seemed like a never-ending line for milking, as we arrived at Ballymakeigh House. Margaret and Michael Browne's lovely 300-year-old Farmhouse has won every award in the book and continues to do so. Not just has the house won awards but Margaret, who is Cork's answer to Superwoman, has been Housewife of the Year, T.V. Chef and published her own best selling cookery book "Through My Kitchen Window". Ballymakeigh is a fun place because Margaret and Mike are absolutely irrepressible loving nothing more than a bit of hilarity. This is a very interesting old house which has calming bedrooms with, as Margaret might say herself, "bags of old fashioned comfort", and of course, perfectly fitted and kitted out en suite bathrooms. If you are feeling energetic, there is a hard tennis court, or you can walk the land, see the milking parlour, or merely sit down in the lovely big conservatory for the day with a glass in hand – nobody will bat an eyelid. Americans love to visit "real Irish" homes and this I can tell you is a "real Irish" home, but with everything running to perfection down to the ice machine. A spanking dinner is served in the lovely old world diningroom. Breakfasts are hearty with fresh pressed apple juice, fruits and yoghurts, traditional grainy porridge with spices, cereals, kippers with thyme, and a super "Full Irish" including rashers, sausages, Clonakilty pudding tomatoes and eggs. Preserves, of course, are homemade as are the breads – traditional

Irish soda bread and leek and onion savoury scones are to die for. Mark my words, like me, you will go back again and again to Ballymakeigh.

Owners:	Michael and Margaret Browne
Address:	Killeagh, Co. Cork.
Tel	024 95184
No. Of Rooms	6
Price	
Double/Twin	€120 - €130
Single	€75
Family	On request
Dinner	Yes
Open	All Year
Credit Cards	Visa MC Amex
Directions	Located 1 mile of N25. 22 miles east of Cork City. Signposted in Killeagh village at Old Thatch Pub.
Email:	ballymakeigh@eircom.net
Web:	www.lucindaosullivan.com/ballymakeighhouse

Baltimore Bay Guesthouse

I t's many a long year now since the legendary Youen Jacob Snr set sail from his native Brittany and landed on the shores of Ireland. He married and opened his Chez Youen restaurant in the little fishing village of Baltimore, West Cork, concentrating on shellfish the simple way that it was served in his native France and the rest, as they say, is history. He has continued to enthrall diners with big platters of jumbo Galley Head prawns, Sherkin Island Oysters and lobster for years and has played host to hundreds of well-known names from here and abroad.

Baltimore is an enchanting village straight out of the Pirates of Penzance or the Caribbean – but it is just more beautiful in West Cork. It is magic and has to be experienced. The village attracts such a diverse and colourful cross section of visitors that it has a unique atmosphere. Baltimore is your oyster whether you want to swim, dive, fish, sail, whale watch, dolphin watch, island-hop or simply sit in the square and watch the sun go down in splendour over the harbour and Mount Gabriel.

Youen's family are now grown

and actively involved in the business with Youen Jnr opening a fab casual continental style café on The Square called La Jolie Brise as well as the super Baltimore Bay Guest House, which is in a stunning location overlooking the harbour.

The bedrooms are understated chic, furnished in a contemporary classy style with well-chosen antique pieces, which intermingle charmingly with the cool modern furniture and feel of this boutique guesthouse. Walls are cool cream, the rooms are a good size, bed linen is crisp and fresh, there are televisions with videos, direct dial phones, and you are right smack in the middle of things. Step next door and have a drink in the Jacob family's Waterfront Bar. Sit down outside the door, and take in the sun and the atmosphere whilst you have your cappuccino, or later in the day delicious pizzas and pastas, grilled fish or vegetarian dishes.

Breakfast can be continental or the Full Irish - whatever is your choice – they also offer fish plus delicious hot chocolate. You can bring the family – they have five family rooms and you can also bring Fido.

It's cool.

Owner	Youen Jacob
Address	The Waterfront, Baltimore, Co. Cork.
Tel:	028 20600
No of Rooms	8
Price	
Double/twin	€80 - €120
Single	€60-80
Family	Enquire (children under 4 sharing room free)
Dinner	La Jolie Brise or Chez Youen
Open	All Year
Credit Cards	Yes
Directions	Take the N71 from Cork to Skibbereen and follow the R595 to Baltimore.
Email	baltimorebay@youenjacob.com
Web	www.lucindaosullivan.com/youenjacob.com

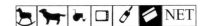

Baltimore Harbour Hotel

Baltimore is a fishing village at the very south of Ireland, spectacularly located looking out to Roaringwater Bay and the Carbery Islands. It is about as far south and out into the water as you can get. A magnet for the "yachties", particularly in July and August during regatta time, so accommodation is at a premium. In Baltimore there is a Sailing Club, two Sailing Schools and two Diving Schools and water is the key word here. Whilst the "junior yachties" are learning the ropes, Mum and Dad can relax and enjoy the local amenities and facilities at The Baltimore Harbour Hotel. Ideally located overlooking the harbour, the Hotel has 64 lovely bedrooms, a 16m swimming pool, bubble pool, children's pool, as well as a sauna, steam room, and treatment rooms for massage and reflexology. I really loved the two and three bedroomed courtyard suites at the Hotel. These suites are not self catering but do have a spacious lounge/kitchen area with a kettle, fridge and microwave and some have balconies. We stayed with our two teenage sons and found the "suite" idea wonderful because when we wanted to socialize in the hotel they could stay behind and watch TV without just being confined to a bedroom. Food at the hotel's Clipper Restaurant is excellent using the best of local West Cork fresh produce and plenty of seafood – think Crab Claw Salad with Citrus dressing or Fresh Tuna Steak on a bed of squid ink Tagliatelle with tomato Herb Sauce. The staff are very friendly and obliging and will cater for all needs and they have a comprehensive children's menu. There are a number of interesting pubs and cafes in Baltimore and ferries leave each day to Cape Clear, which has incredible bird life, and for Sherkin Island which has two lovely sandy beaches. The hotel's Chartroom Bar has music sessions in summer and at weekends or alternatively you might enjoy sitting in the local square with a

cool drink watching the sun go down over the islands. Paradise Regained.

Owners:	Charles Cullinane.
Address:	Baltimore, Co. Cork.
Tel	028 20361
No. Of Rooms	64
Price	
Double/Twin	From €140 +(Special Rates available throughout the year on request from hotel)
Single	From €90
Family	€180 (2 Adults + 2 Children)
Dinner	Yes - Restaurant
Open	February – 21st December
Credit Cards	All Major Cards
Directions	Signposted on the right on entry to Baltimore
Email	info@baltimoreharbourhotel.ie
Web	www.lucindaosullivan.com/baltimoreharbouthotel

Bayview Hotel

Ballycotton is a completely unspoiled Fishing Village in East Cork dating back to 1250 AD. Not only is it completely unspoiled but it is also largely undiscovered save by those in the know, for people tend to dash on further west to the overblown more high profile villages. Once you turn down at Castlemartyr you whirl around the back roads amongst high hedges and fertile fields which are eons away from the modern world – and yet so near. Ballycotton is an ideal base for visiting Cork, if you prefer to stay out of a City, or for taking a leisurely tour of Stephen Pearce's Pottery and for visiting Ballymaloe, and the Jameson Irish Whiskey Centre at Midleton, after which you might need to be careful on the Ballycotton Cliff Walk!!

BAYVIEW HOTEL BALLYCOTTON

I have had a problem for a number of years with Hotels and Restaurants a problem which can spoil one's entire visit – namely – the "back room" and the "table beside the toilet door respectively. I have been offered a far from romantic attic in Paris, a box in London beside a lift shaft with pneumatic drills working in it, no sea view all over the place, a room over the rubbish exit in Palma, and even rooms with no view at all save the sidewall of the next building. The Bayview Hotel in my eyes is just perfectly designed for all the rooms have magnificent sea views. As you look out it feels more like a "visual tour" because you are just over the sheer drop onto the rocks, gazing out into infinity, broken only by the old world little quaint Ballycotton Harbour. Not only does the newly revamped Bayview have 35 perfect rooms, a comfortable library style bar and lounge, it has excellent food provided by Head Chef, Ciaran Scully, who cooks up the best of luscious French style food in The Capricho Restaurant in this special little gourmet Hotel. Think prawns the size of your thumb and silky foie gras … There are six golf

courses within 30 minutes drive, as well as some of the best sea angling in Europe. Stephen Belton provides a 5 star service at the 4 star Bayview. Go and discover it for yourself.

Owners	John & Carmel O'Brien
	Stephen Belton (General Manager)
Address	Ballycotton, Co. Cork.
Tel	021 4646746
No. Of Rooms	35
Price	
Double /Twin	From €125 Room Only
Single	From €125 Room Only
Family	From €125 Room Only
Dinner	Yes - Restaurant
Open	Mid April to end October
Credit Cards	All Major Cards
Directions	Located in Ballycotton Village
Email	res@thebayviewhotel.com
Web	www.lucindaosullivan.com/bayviewhotel

The Blue Haven Hotel

I was at the very first Kinsale Gourmet Festival in the mid 70's when it was a fledgling event but, like Topsy, it just growed and growed, along with it Kinsale's reputation worldwide on the foodie scene. A pivotal part of this foodie arena has always been the Blue Haven Hotel, which was run like a very tight ship and into which everybody seemed to report at some part of the day. We have had great nights there with people from all over the world in Kinsale for shark fishing, the food, sailing or just the fun of the whole place. In fact on one occasion we had such an hilarious stay it took us three days to leave! We got up each morning with the best of intentions but, we would meet someone we knew, and after a couple of "farewell" jars couldn't set off to drive to Dublin so, back we would have to go to Reception, and beg for our room, or any room!

Local guy, Ciaran Fitzgerald, is now at the helm of the Blue Haven and has spent the past two years revamping and restoring it into a very fine atmospheric and welcoming Boutique type Hotel. All of the very stylish bedrooms have had a major face lift to bring them in line with the requirements of today's discerning traveller - flat screen TV's, those really expensive beds, pillow menus, wild wood furniture, wireless broadband and spanking newly fitted bathrooms.

There is a new relaxed bistro restaurant now in situ called Blu with an outdoor deck and pre dinner drinks area. The food is modern, well executed and just what is wanted nowadays. You can think perhaps of lobster, scallops, or prawns, partnered with good Mediterranean vegetables, asparagus, artichokes, aubergines and followed by scrumptious puds. There is food all over the place at the Blue Haven for there is also the more informal dining option in the Bar, Conservatory and a deck area called The Fishmarket complete with outdoor heaters and an overhead canopy. Really good food is available all day so if you want to be at the hub in Kinsale – The Blue Haven is the place to be – you never know if you are lucky it might take you 3 days to check out!

 NET

Owners	Ciaran Fitzgerald
Address	Pearse Street, Kinsale, Co. Cork.
Tel	021 4772209
No. Of Rooms	17
Price	
Double/Twin	From €195
Single	From €140
Family	From €230
Dinner	Yes – Restaurant, Bar Food and Coffee Shop
Open	All Year
Credit Cards	Visa MC Amex Laser
Directions	Follow signs for the South Link and the airport and you will join the R27. After passing Cork Airport, three miles further on at the Five-Mile-Bridge take the R600 to Kinsale Town.
Email	info@bluehavenkinsale.com
Web	www.lucindaosullivan.com/bluehaven

Crawford House

I don't know about you but I have ended up in foreign cities wishing I knew of some gorgeous place to rest my head. I ended up one time in an attic in Paris in a street lined with prostitutes and I was absolutely petrified. On another occasion I ended up in London in a dreary hotel with a bedroom beside the lift shaft – that wasn't too bad save that the lift was out of order and being repaired with pneumatic drills going 24/7. If you are in bad accommodation you are not only miserable but it completely colours your view of the City you are in.

My Cork City gem is Crawford House which has it all – quality – distinction – style – contemporary ambience. On top of that it has a location that is second to none being in the City's University area – in fact it is just across from the College. Two Gothic revival style tall imperious Victorian houses have been converted into a slick modern home away from home by Cork girl Cecilia O'Leary and her husband Hossayn providing all the facilities the modern day traveller wants.

There are 12 beautiful bedrooms with oakwood furniture custom made by the same crafts people who furnished U2's uber chic Clarence Hotel in

Dublin. There are superking orthopaedic beds, even for single occupancy, cool crisp bedlinen, all modern facilities, satellite television, and modem and fax points for the business traveller. The bathrooms are pristine and elegant with Jacuzzi baths and power showers,

There is a comfortable serene lounge in which to relax and breakfast next morning is served in the cool diningroom and conservatory. You can of course have the de rigueur Full Irish but there is also a lavish buffet of cereals, fruit, compotes, breads as well as pancakes, omelettes, confitures. Hossayn is a great cook with a light hand and everybody just loves his breakfasts. Most importantly, if you have a dietary requirement, they will, with advance notice of course, be more than happy to cater for you.

Crash out at Crawford House ... you will have found your new base in Cork.

Owners	Cecilia O'Leary Kareem
Address	Western Road, Cork.
Tel:	021 4279000
No of Rooms	12
Price	
Double/twin	€110-€120
Single	€80
Family	
Dinner	No
Open	January 15 – December 15
Credit Cards	Yes
Directions	From central Cork follow signs for Western Road. Facing UCC.
Email	info@crawfordhouse.ie
Web	

www.lucindaosullivan.com/crawfordhouse

Friar's Lodge

The first time I met Maureen Tierney we had arrived with two small boys in the car, hot, tired and ratty. Jack Charlton was the Irish Soccer Team Manager, it was "Ole Ole Year"- 1990 when Ireland took the summer off to support the Irish Team in the World Cup. We were renting a self-catering house from her. She strolled up the street smiling and cool, immediately lowering our stress levels – nothing seemed to faze her and nothing was a problem

Maureen Tierney has always been ahead of the game. In recent years, various luxury B & Bs and Guesthouses have come on stream in Kinsale and they may well be very excellent but some are also very expensive, catering for wealthy golfers coming to play at the Old Head. Maureen said to herself "what about providing luxury accommodation but at reasonable prices" and Friar's Lodge was born.

In the centre of town, nothing is lacking for Maureen's specifications were meticulous for her new venture which is proving a real winner. Friar's Lodge is built over and around a central archway, leading to ample private parking and three self-catering houses. The rooms and suites are like good hotel rooms, spacious, with all creature comforts, turn down service, choccies on your pillow – a pillow menu – telephone, TV, DVD, radio, internet connection, safe, ironing centre, mini bar available, and of course an elevator. You can also bring your pet – but do enquire first cos that doesn't include elephants or alligators!

There are lovely relaxing lounge areas where you can sit and chat with

other guests or read the magazines. Maureen and her staff provide that extra 4 Star Service and will make any reservations you wish or arrange tee times – there is also a drying room for golfers. There is a compact wine menu available to residents and complimentary sherry sits in the decanter just waiting for you to have that aperitif before you toddle out to one of the many famous Kinsale restaurants. Breakfasts are delicious – help yourself to the cereals, fruits, and juices and then have a hot breakfast. "Would you like some fish," said Maureen, "we just run down to the local fish shop – which is particularly good – and bring it in fresh........."

Nothing is ever too much trouble for Maureen Tierney – she is still smiling and unflappable – outstanding – loves horses and is definitely in the winner's enclosure.

Owners	Maureen Tierney
Address	Friar's Street, Kinsale, Co. Cork.
Tel	021 4777384
No. Of Rooms	18
Price	
Suite/Family	€140 Children under 5 free.
Double/Twin	€120
Single	€80
Dinner	No – Kinsale is awash with restaurants.
Open	All Year – Closed 22nd – 28th December.
Credit Cards	Visa MC Amex Laser

Directions.	Follow signs for the South Link and the airport and you will join the R27. After passing Cork Airport, three miles further on at the Five-Mile-Bridge take the R600 to Kinsale Town.
Email:	mtierney@indigo.ie
Web:	www.lucindaosullivan.com/friarslodge

Garryvoe Hotel

G arryvoe in East Cork is to scores of Corkonians what Skerries is to Dubliners, and maybe what Long Island was to New Yorkers– where the childhood holidays were spent. Long innocent days on the beach, simple fun in rented summer houses or caravans, sand in the banana sandwiches and romps through the rough grass with Fido, beach balls, rounders and windbreakers, it was not in any way sophisticated. Fond memories.

For Irish people along with those memories of Skerries, Garryvoe, and sand filled sandwiches, is the taste of those wonderful Dublin Bay Prawns - which we took for granted – great big bruisers that our parents used to buy straight from the Fishing boats, pop in the boiling water for a flash and eat with salt and mayonnaise. They are nearly a thing of the past on Irish menus now, replaced by every old excuse of a prawn from distant shores, but I can let you in on a secret – at the Garryvoe Hotel you will also find them on the menu in bucket loads – Prawn Cocktail – the real thing – Prawns with Garlic Butter – the real thing – Prawn Scampi – the real thing – Prawns Mornay – you haven't seen that in a while have you?

The Garryvoe Hotel was for many years a solid country hotel but has been transformed into a magnificent new establishment with superb bedrooms and suites overlooking the beach. It has a swish new diningroom complete with twinkling ceiling, and smart new bar. We were in a glorious Junior Suite with a wonderful high cathedral ceiling - I could have stayed in that room for a week without leaving it – and lived on room service. It was so cool and calming with a giant sized bed, beautiful big brown sofas, clear white walls, blue curtains and a view of the sea that seemed never ending. We left the balcony doors open all night to hear the lapping of the waves – it was just bliss.

There is a generosity of spirit too in The Garryvoe both with Stephen Belton, the General Manager, and properietors, John and Carmel O'Brien, who also own the Bayview Hotel in Ballycotton. Garryvoe is just beside Ballymaloe and Shannagarry and is a superb place to stay.

Owners	Stephen Belton, General Manager.
Address	Garryvoe, Castlemartyr, East Cork.
Tel	021 4646718
No. Of Rooms	48
Price	
Double/Twin	From €69 Room Only
Single	From €69 Room Only
Family	From €69 Room Only
Dinner	Yes - Restaurant
Open	All Year
Credit Cards	Visa MC Amex Diners Laser
Directions.	In the heart of Garryvoe village facing the beach
Email:	res@garryvoehotel.com
Web:	www.lucindaosullivan.com/garryvoe

NET H P

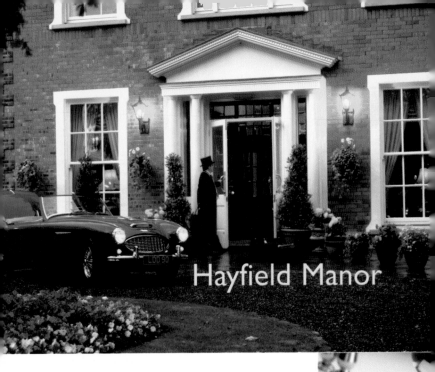

Hayfield Manor

"Thelma and Louise" said the General Manager, of the 5 Star Hayfield Manor Hotel welcoming and helping the windblown disheveled pair scramble out of the low open topped car with their bags. It is not very often that the General Manager of any Hotel is at the door to greet one – they are usually hiding away in their Offices leaving the front of house stuff to their minions. I must say it was very impressive and this hands on approach clearly results in a very high standard of performance all round. Hayfield Manor, a member of the Small Luxury Hotels of the World, is where the Legal fraternity rest their briefs when in Cork – and believe me they like their comforts. A red bricked neo-Georgian building set in two acres of ground with mature trees and surrounded by a 15-foot wall. Located beside the University it has a magnificent new Spa, along with shimmering Pool and Beauty Salon just for residents' use. The first impression is "oh, its so pretty" – like a Connecticut Mansion in an American movie – everything perfect with a lovely old picturesque tree right outside the front door, topiary planters, carriage lights, and a liveried doorman. The bedrooms are beautifully draped and lavishly furnished and I got to sleep in the suite used by Pierce Brosnan and his wife just after they departed! I felt like I never wanted to leave it. This is where anyone who is anyone stays when they come to Cork. There is an air of being cushioned away from the real world at Hayfield and, although it is 5 star, it is absolutely unpretentious.

56

Fabulous food is served in Orchids Restaurant - foie gras parfait, scallops, turbot, lamb, organic duck breast and so on whilst in the lovely new light and airy conservatory style fashionable Perrot's Restaurant there is a superb selection of modern food at very reasonable prices. There is of course further pampering available at The Beautique at Hayfield Manor which offers superb Elemis Spa Therapy in male and female treatment rooms. It is the ultimate urban retreat. Hayfield, a wonderful luxurious oasis in Cork, only a mile from Patrick Street and is the perfect place for business or pleasure. Enquire too about their special breaks. I just want to live permanently in the picture postcard world of Hayfield Manor. Special Offers are available throughout the year so do contact the hotel re those rates.

Owners	Joe and Margaret Scally
Address	Hayfield Manor, Perrott Avenue, College Road, Cork.
Tel	021 4845900
No. Of Rooms	88
Price	
	Suites From €475
Double	€380
Twin	€380
Single	€380
Dinner	Yes – 2 Restaurants
Open	All Year
Credit Cards	Visa MC Amex Diners Laser
Directions	Signed off College Road
Email:	enquiries@hayfieldmanor.ie
Web:	www.lucindaosullivan.com/hayfieldmanor

Hotel Isaacs

The idea for Hotel Isaac's was inspired. A vast, red bricked, Victorian landmark building on Cork's MacCurtain Street, used by Nat Ross Removals, was converted into Hotel Isaac's, offering great value accommodation in excellent surroundings.

While the Hotel itself is an oasis of calm its Bar and Greene's Restaurant are very popular with those in the know seeking good food. But more of that later. The bedrooms are extremely comfortable, bright and airy, and ideal for the technophile and modern day traveller requiring Internet access, safes, minibars, transcontinental built in adaptors, airconditioning, trouser press, iron and ironing boards. The locatrion is brilliant for Hotel Isaacs is a few minutes from Cork's Kent Station, is surrounded by restaurants, clubs, pubs, boutiques and antique and décor shops.

Greene's, the Hotel's own Brasserie Restaurant, is under the baton of French chef, Frederic Deformeau. It overlooks a floodlit cascading feature waterfall so you are ideally placed for a fun gourmet weekend. The food is excellent and you can think perhaps of lovely fresh timbale of crab with avocado, lemon and chive mayonnaise, topped with toasted brioche or French Chavignol goat's cheese stuffed with semi-dried tomato and black olives, wrapped in Parma ham and served on spicy red onion bruschetta

drizzled with balsamic and olive oil. One of my favourite dishes there is a parcel of Savoy cabbage, filled with an excellent duck confit and vegetable brunoise served on spicy Puy lentils with a rich deep red wine jus. That always makes my trip to Greene's worth while – a little bit of rustic France in the Rebel County. Mains include excellent shellfish, shank of lamb on confit roast potatoes and much much more.

There are also 11 excellent two and three bedroomed apartments adjacent ot the Hotel which are very popular and suitable for small groups, families and business people who like a bit more space and freedom.

At Hotel Isaacs you are in the heart of Cork.

Owners	Paula Lynch (General Manager)
Address	48 MacCurtain Street, Cork.
Tel:	021 450 0011
No of Rooms	61
Price	
Double/twin	€80 - €260
Single	€70 - €200
2/3 Bed Apts	€700 - €1050 per week
Dinner	Yes – Restaurant and Barfood
Open	All year save Christmas
Credit Cards	Yes
Directions	From Patrick Street follow directions to Cork Railway Station. Hotel on left in one way traffic system.
Email	cork@isaacs.ie
Web	www.lucindaosullivan.com/hotelisaacscork

Kilfinnan Farmhouse

long the south west coastline of West Cork which is a myriad of little bays and creeks, sandy coves, tidal loughs and magical ocean sprays is Glandore, a glorious coastal tiny village comprising a little harbour, a couple of pubs, a small hotel, and a Restaurant high on the hill. So enticing is Glandore that it surely got separated from its Italian mother during the ice age landing instead on Irish shores to bring a little continental glamour. It is spectacularly beautiful and a magnet for wealthy Dublin and Cork people. Glandore is relatively undiscovered by Tourists who "don't turn down" but keep going on the main road through Leap (pronounced Lep) like the clappers heading further West not realizing that the whole point of West Cork and Kerry is to amble and socialise, not race through it. They don't know what they are missing. The two pubs that pretty well make up Glandore have tables by a low wall on this natural "terrace" but if you don't get there early in the summertime you have had it. The whole point about Glandore is not just to admire the view but to "people watch". You sit there, with your friends, enjoying pretty sandwiches from "Hayes Bar" for as long as possible, observing the top of the range cars and their drivers cruise slowly through …

KILFINNAN FARMHOUSE

Accommodation in Glandore is at a premium but just an Irish mile away, high up overlooking Glandore Harbour, is Margaret Mehigan's lovely family run Kilfinnan Farmhouse which, apart from being lovely, offers super, very reasonably priced, accommodation. The sweet old ivy clad house has four en suite bedrooms with really comfortable beds, crisp bedlinen and pretty views, some overlooking the old world garden. You are likely to meet Margaret's sister in law, Ann, bringing the cows in for milking as you arrive whilst Margaret, meantime, envelopes you in the warmth of her welcome. Don't expect foil-covered butters and shop bought marmalade at Kilfinnan. Everything is beautifully presented in pretty dishes and the milk, eggs, meat,

fruit and vegetables are freshly produced on the farm so you can only benefit. Last time I was there I watched a Spanish family try porridge with honey and whiskey – in fact they tried everything in sight – delicious fruit salads..the Full Irish … it was all so different for them ..and they loved it. Kilfinnan is surrounded by pretty little beaches which for the most part of the year are virtually unoccupied. There are all sorts of water based activities nearby – water-skiing, sailing, and diving down to look at all the wrecks which came a cropper. The stunningly impressive Bronze Age Drombeg stone circle, made up of a formation of seventeen stones, is just across the fields leading down to the water. Nearby there is also a fulacht fiadh, which is an ancient cooking site where troughs of water would have been heated by hot stones thrown into them from a fire. Kilfinnan Farm is a real find in a real Ireland – don't tell anyone – oh and you will have free highspeed Broadband aceess too.

Owner	Margaret Mehigan
Address	Kilfinnan Farm, Glandore, Co. Cork.
Tel	028 33233
No. Of Rooms	4
Price	
Double	€90
Twin	€90
Single	€55
Family	Negotiable (Children under 4 free. Discount under 14's)
Dinner	High Tea available
Open	All Year
Credit Cards	No
Directions.	Take R597 to Glandore. Watch for signpost to left for house.
Email	kilfinnanfarm@eircom.net
Web	www.lucindaosullivan.com/kilfinnanfarm

Knockeven House

obh, as most people know, was the final departure point of the ill-fated Titanic Liner on its maiden voyage to New York in 1912. Not only is it a nostalgic town for that reason but, for thousands of Irish people, Cobh (formerly known as Queenstown) was the last image of Ireland as they emigrated to America with many never returning to their native land.. It is quite a spectacular image to retain in one's memory for, sailing out of Cobh Harbour, looking back at the houses stacked up the hill under the spire of the elaborate almost fairy tale neo Gothic, Pugin designed, Cathedral is particularly beautiful.

Thousands of people visit Cobh each year to retrace the footsteps of their ancestors and to visit the wonder Cobh Heritage Centre. Strangely enough I have to confess that I did not discover Knockeven House myself - although I am often in that area – I heard about it from somebody living in New York who contacted me to tell me how wonderful it was …. and it is.

I am pathologically fussy about where I stay because it can make such a difference to the enjoyment of one's entire holiday but believe me if you stay at John and Pam Mulhaire's beautiful home you will not only enjoy it you will

be suitably impressed and enchanted all at once. Knockeven House was built in 1840 and the graciousness of the era is evident all over this splendid house. This has been Pam and John's home for twenty years but they have only recently totally and lavishly revamped the house with incredible style and taste and opened it up to guests. We were very impressed and dying to know where the beautiful wallpapers and fabrics used throughout had been sourced. The hall and landing is splendid and imposing, the drawingroom magnificent and gracious, whilst the beautiful diningroom overlooks the conservatory. The oversized bedrooms are divine and Pam's kitchen is straight out of House & Garden. To add to all of this magnificence, Pam and John are delightful. Pam chatters away and John is a good man for amusing stories when he is not out minding his beautiful gardens.

Knockeven House offers superb glorious accommodation at a fraction of the cost of similar accommodation in a top Hotel and is perfect also for visiting Cork City as you are over the river on the little ferry in a few minutes and you can also whiz out on the South Ring to West Cork.

Owners	John and Pam Mulhaire
Address:	Rushbrooke,
	Cobh,
	Co. Cork
Tel	021 4811778
No. Of Rooms	4
Price	
Double/Twin	€120 - €130
Single	€75 - €80
Family	€150
Dinner	No
Open	1st February – 2nd January
Credit Cards	Visa MC
Directions	From Cork. N25 in direction Rosslare Waterford. Take Cobh exit R624. Pass Fota Wildlife Park over the bridge. Turn left at The Great Island Garage. First right avenue to Knockeven House.
Email	info@knockevenhouse.com
Web	www.knockevenhouse.com

KINSALE

My favourite place in the whole world is undoubtedly Kinsale. The first time I went away from home with a group of friends on a Bank Holiday skite it was to Kinsale. I spent my honeymoon in Kinsale, my eldest son took his first steps in Kinsale, I will probably end up in Kinsale. The pretty narrow streets are lined with historic old houses, colourful shops and galleries, great bars, and great places to eat. Stroll down Pier Road by the new marina, take a trip out on the water. You just won't find another Kinsale anywhere else in the world.

Old Bank House

During the years I have seen many of the good people who put Kinsale firmly on the world map retire and take life a little more easily. A town to be vibrant and maintain its good reputation has to have fresh blood in its arteries who will bring it forward – as far as Kinsale is now concerned – local chap Ciaran Fitzgerald is one such person. Ciaran has recently embraced the beautiful Old Bank House as part of his group, The Blue Haven Collection, which also owns the nearby super Blue Haven Hotel.

The Old Bank House is a magnificent Georgian House right smack in the middle of all the activity in Kinsale. It has been lavishly revamped from top to toe with the most magnificent fabrics, drapes, throws, bedcovers, fine antiques and original paintings. Most of the individually designed

bedrooms have views of the harbour and town and they really are superb so if you want lush plush luxury – and who doesn't – the Old Bank House is for you ... and me.

What I like about the Old Bank House too is that after you have meandered around the shops and the bars, you can just stroll back in and crash out in a squishy sofa in the lovely drawingroom, read the paper, have a glass of wine, relax, you are on your holidays. After a great nights sleep in those big comfortable beds, you will be ready for the beautifully set out Breakfast Room. There is a lavish buffet selection with probiotic Greek yogurt, a platter of freshly cut seasonal fruit and berries, local cheeses, fruit compotes, traditional oatmeal porridge, scrambled eggs with smoked salmon, omelettes ...

The Old Bank House is "doing Kinsale" in style.

Owners	Ciaran Fitzgerald
Address	11 Pearse Street, Kinsale, Co. Cork.
Tel	021 4774075
No of Rooms	17
Price	
Double	From €195
Twin	From €230
Family	From €230
Dinner	No – but sister hotel just beside it.
Open	All Year
Credit Cards	Yes
Directions	On arrival into Kinsale, there is a junction. The Old Bank House Is directly on the right, on the main street.
Email	info@oldbankhousekinsale.com
Web	www.lucindaosullivan.com/oldbankhouse

Radisson SAS Hotel & Spa, Cork

When I read "Sensual Chocolate Wrap", I immediately thought, that sounds tasty. Well, it is, but not in an edible way. The wrap, made with real cocoa, is a luxurious chocolate body wrap – every woman's dream - and is one of the many treatments available in the luxurious Retreat Spa and Fitness Centre in the Radisson SAS Hotel and Spa at Little Island , which uses Elemis products and also has a unique Hydrotherapy Treatment Pool. Ditchley House, a 19th century listed building, has been lavishly restored and the Radisson was built adjacent to the victorian house and opened its welcoming doors to the public on the 21st June 2005.

Just beside Cork City, and conveniently located to Cork International Airport, the Hotel is everything one would expect from a Radisson SAS operation. There are 129 ensuite rooms – deluxe suites, business class rooms, and family rooms, all beautifully styled and luxuriously furnished in Urban and Ocean style. All rooms have 24 hour room service, one touch direct dial telephones, plasma screen TVs, in house movie channels, mini-bar, tea or coffee hospitality tray, in room safe, trouser press incorporating iron and ironing board, and free WIFI internet access. With all such accessories you may never wish to leave your room.

But there is more. The Banks Bar is the destination after a long business meeting or an afternoon in the Spa. Relax and enjoy one of the creative cocktails on offer. They have a very

good bar menu and also for dining, just off the bar, is the Island Grill Room which does things like a really decent fish pie as well as warm cracked crab claws, confit duck leg with Lyonnaise potates or maybe ravioli filled with asparagus and ricotta cheese at good prices. They really push out the boat for breakfast with a superb buffet with up to 63 mouth watering items to choose from.

The hotel's conference and meeting facilites are second to none – up to date in room equipment and services and anything else required, and their detailed information packs mean you can select and dictate what you want and expect, and you won't be disappointed.

Whether it is business, a spa break, or a weekend in Cork, the new Radisson SAS is fab.

Owners	Ruairi O'Connor (General Manager)
Address	Ditchley House, Little Island, Cork.
Tel:	021 4297000
No of Rooms	129
Price	
Executive Suite	€205
Double/twin	€140

Single	€140
Family	€250
Dinner	Yes – Restaurant and Bar food
Open	All Year
Credit Cards	Yes
Directions	East of Cork City. From Dunkettle Interchange roundabout, take 3rd exit signed Rosslare/Waterford. 1 mile on, take slip road for Little Island. Cross flyover, take 3rd exit off roundabout. Hotel is 1st entrance on right.
Email	info.cork@radissonsas.com
Web	

www.lucindaosullivan.com/corkradissonsas

Sea View House Hotel

"**Y**es, we do breakfast in bed ... if necessary," said the wonderful Miss Kathleen O'Sullivan, Proprietress of the Sea View House Hotel at Ballylickey, in response to my timorous enquiry on the telephone the night before. We felt like two naughty schoolgirls – but yes, they did breakfast in bed all right and, as one would expect under Kathleen O'Sullivan's eagle eye, it arrived on the button of 8 a.m. and was just perfect. It is no wonder that this much loved haven of hospitality won the AA Courtesy and Care Award. A new wing was added not so long ago to the Seaview House, along with a magnificent French classical style round "conservatory" to the dining room, and it is just a fab place to stay. All of the

rooms are splendid with larger rooms being absolutely divine – some opening out to the gardens – beautifully furnished with antiques, French Armoires and headboards, wonderful paintings – each different and each special We had arrived like two exhausted rats into the hall of the Seaview, having driven in and out of every peninsula from Cork to Ballylickey. Make no

mistake this takes hours, but I don't feel I have had my fix of West Cork each summer without doing it. Having showered and dickied ourselves up we went down the corridor past Kathleen O'Sullivan's "Command Centre". "You look very nice", she said to my companion – "go through that door there and you can have a drink". Having passed muster we went into a cocktail bar and armed ourselves with suitable sherries and set down to peruse the menus. The food is excellent – think Sauté Lamb kidneys Madeira sauce, whisper light Scampi or avocado with real Dublin Bay Prawns, Rack of Lamb or lemon sole all perfectly produced and served. "Do we get both Puddings and Cheese?" asked a young Englishman sitting across from us with his wife. His eyes lighting up like a child's when given the affirmative answer. We all looked together at a Victor Meldrew look-alike who passed by us and the young man said "we feel very young" – "so do we", we chimed sharply to this mere fresh faced youth. The Seaview House Hotel is brilliant – you will absolutely love it.

Owners:	Kathleen O'Sullivan
Address:	Ballylickey, Bantry, Co. Cork.
Tel	027 50073
No. Of Rooms	25
Price	
Mini Suite	€175 - €200
Double	€140 - €165
Twin	€140 - €165
Single	€90
Family	€150 - €170
Dinner	Yes
Open	Mid March to Mid November
Credit Cards	All Major Cards
Directions.	Located on main Bantry to Glengarriff road.
Email:	info@seaviewhousehotel.com
Web:	
www.lucindaosullivan.com/seaviewhousehotel	

Shearwater

Without a doubt, Kinsale is on the itinerary of pretty well every tourist who comes to our shores, be they foodies or yachtties, or just plain wanting to visit this pretty town, which has achieved world wide fame. We went on our honeymoon to Kinsale and have been up and down a few times every year since to this gorgeous romantic town with its narrow colourful streets and myriad of restaurants. There is always a buzz in Kinsale – be it winter or summer – in fact we like it even better out of season.

Right on the marina, just beside Kinsale Yacht Club, is Shearwater, a new development of exclusive magnificent apartments and duplexes in what is probably the most stunning location in Ireland, never mind Kinsale, unrivalled and unprecedented.

Available for short-term letting in Shearwater is a magnificent duplex,

which very comfortably sleeps up to four people. The steps up to the front entrance bring you into your own little world that is so modern and airy that it has the feel and panache of a New York loft. The first floor has two bedrooms. The very spacious master bedroom, which is ensuite, has a super kingsize bed, which can convert to two singles. The guest bedroom has two single beds and both have views of the harbour.

Upstairs leads you to the most amazing enormous room with high Cathedral ceiling and velux windows. There is a bay window at one end with views of the boats and out over the roof tops of Kinsale. It is very stylishly furnished with eclectic Franco Chinese furnishings. The kitchen area is beautifully constructed and fitted with everything anyone could possibly want. There is private secure car parking and on the ground level is Vista a coffee/wine bar so you just nip downstairs and pick up your croissants for breakfast. Live the dream – you won't want to leave.

Owners	Mary Morris
Address	Shearwater, Kinsale, Co. Cork.
Tel	087 2513249
No of Rooms	Sleeps 4
Price	€695 - €995 per week
Dinner	Self-Catering
Open	All Year
Credit Cards	Yes
Directions	On Marina
Email	tsar@eircom.net
Web	www.lucindaosullivan.com/shearwater

Sheraton Fota Island
Golf Resort & Spa

Fota Island just east of Cork City is one of the most beautiful places in Ireland. It is best known for its Wildlife Park, which is a joint project between the Zoological Society of Ireland and University College Cork. It is a wonderful opportunity to see many endangered species from lemurs to zebras up close and personal with very little restriction.

Last year saw the opening of the stunning new Sheraton Fota Island Golf Resort & Spa. The location is fab right beside this wonderful nature reserve, only 10 minutes to Cork City, close to Cobh and the Titanic trail. Nip on the little car-ferry across the bay, and you are into West Cork and Kinsale in half an hour. The Hotel itself is a low rise building sitting at the top of a hill overlooking parklands and the golf course and there is just that wonderful feel of being away from it all … and somewhere special. There is an almost Hispanic feel to the large lobby with its beamed ceiling, stone columns, marble floors and oak furnishings. Off the lobby is a beautiful big bar leading to the Fota restaurant serving excellent food. There is also a fine dining

seafood grillroom, The Cove, tucked away beside the wine cellar. The food here is really special but do book in advance as it is not very large. We dined on slivers of Pata Negra filled with fig puree and topped with Parmesan shavings. We followed up with divine scallops on sautéed foie gras and braised pork belly.... and the best ever sole on the bone filled with a Nicoise dressing ... and the puddings - seriously good.

The bedrooms are very stylish with all the de rigueur requirements of today's up market hotels ... great big comfortable beds, lovely bedlinen, mini bar stocked with goodies, plasma TV, internet access, extra large dressing area with his and hers hanging spaces, and a stunning bathroom with big walk in wet room style shower and a big bath as well.

The Island Spa is amazing set in this natural habitat. There are 16 treatment rooms and the whole place is just beautiful. Whether you have a Chocolate Sensualite, Marine Body Polish or a Seacrystal bath .... there is a huge range...you will feel wonderful after it.

Actually I could stay in the Sheraton Fota Island for a week and never move out.

Owners	Paul Dunphy (General Manager)
Address	Fota Island, Cork.
Tel	021 4673000
No of Rooms	131
Price	
Double/twin	From €169
Single	From €169
Family	From €169
Dinner and Barfood	Yes – 2 Restaurants
Open	All Year
Credit Cards	Yes
Directions	Located off the N25 east of Cork City. Take slip road signposted Carrigtohill/Cobh R624. At roundabout take 4th exit. At next Roundabout take 1st exit.
Email	reservations.fota@sheraton.com
Web	www.lucindaosullivan.com/sheraton/cork

Spa NET H 18h P

Inchiquin House

At some stage in our lives we all have a vision of discovering a gorgeous house tucked away in the countryside, as well furnished and as comfortable as our own home, and being able to play house there for a week or two without any of the responsibilities. It is not easy but I have found such a precious gem, Inchiquin House. Michael and Margaret Browne are perfectionists, so the house is lovingly restored. Big and spacious, this Victorian five bedroomed house has beds that are only equalled in comfort with the beds in their other establishment, the nearby Ballymakeigh House. My favourite bedroom is on the ground floor with French doors opening out on to the gardens. The house has four bathrooms and a very functional and pleasant kitchen facing west. The kitchen is the focal point of the house by day and the large sittingroom with open fire is there to while away the night in comfort. There is a very attractive dining area which would be perfect for entertaining friends and family or, alternatively, you can also book yourself into Ballymakeigh

House for dinner. Expect a welcome pack of Ballymakeigh preserves and bread on arrival. Inchiquin House is conveniently located at the end of a tree lined avenue off the N25, twenty miles east of Cork City and two miles from Youghal and is perfect too for visiting Ballymaloe, Midleton, Lismore, and all the surrounding areas.

Owners	Michael and Margaret Browne
Address	Killeagh, Co. Cork.
Tel/Fax	024 95184/024 95370
No. Of Rooms	5
Price	€500 - €800 per week self catering.
Dinner	Available at Ballymakeigh House
Open	All Year
Credit Cards	Visa MC
Directions	Ring for directions

Email: Ballymakeigh@eircom.net
Web: www.lucindaosullivan.com/inchiquin

County Donegal

From the Inishowen peninsula in the north, to the sweeping beaches of the south, Donegal with its two hundred mile coastline has scenery that is unsurpassed throughout the country and is well worth a tour. Enter Donegal from the south through the popular bucket and spade holiday resort of Bundoran and travel north through Laghey before reaching Donegal Town where you may visit O'Donnell Castle. Continue around to Dunkineely with its fabulous St. John's Point and then on to Killybegs, Ireland's most successful fishing village. Onwards and upwards will bring you to Glencolumbcille and its numerous megalithic remains and nearby folk village and museum. Rejoin the N56 which winds its way northwards through Ardara, Glenties, Dungloe, and the Irish speaking Gweedore and Gortahork. The road turns southwards at Dunfanaghy, leave the N56 and go further east to the sweeping Lough Swilly and southwards through Rathmullan, to the pretty Ramelton on the banks of the salmon rich River Leannan. Continue on to Letterkenny, the county's largest town, and site of St. Eunan's Cathedral and onwards to Lifford the county town close to the Northern Ireland border town of Strabane. I should mention that Donegal has the highest seacliffs in Europe at Slieve League. Don't forget the Rosses, an area which includes Kincaslough from whence Ireland's most popular balladeer comes, and where hundreds of people flock every year to his home for the annual tea party with Daniel O'Donnell and his mother.

"A folk singer is someone who sings through his nose by ear"
(ANON)

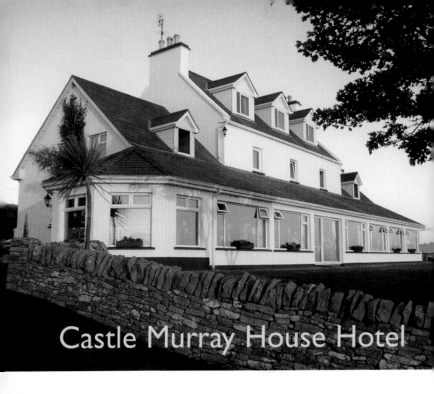

Castle Murray House Hotel

CastleMurray House Hotel is fabulously located on a cliff top, with spectacular sea and stunning coastal views out over McSwyne's Bay, in one of the most dramatic counties in Ireland. Dunkineely has Mountcharles to the east with its sea angling centre and boats available for hire and, to the west, Killybegs, probably Ireland's busiest fishing village. The ruins of McSwyne's Castle are owned by the Hotel and are floodlit at night which adds to an already wonderful inherently brilliant atmosphere. The word Hotel conjures up Modern 4 Star with Leisure Centre but CastleMurray is far more intimate than that – more inns and havens feel - which are not words used very much in Ireland but do describe very well a good Restaurant with excellent accommodation and atmosphere. The ten bedrooms are all en-suite, furnished individually, and have digital T.V. and all facilities. The bathrooms are beautiful having just been recently refurbished. One room is done in African style with black African carved face masks, giraffe cushions with leopard skin lampshades – you can fantasise you are on Safari though I would

prefer to be here in Donegal. Another room has a pretty window seat and is beautifully decorated in colorful coral. CastleMurray is a very comfortable and relaxing spot. Have a jar in the newly refurbished bar before and after dinner – you can relax as you are not going to have to drive anywhere. Meals can be served outside on the verandah

in the Summer. The food is wonderful – pick your own lobster out of a tank – prawns, scallops, crab and don't forget to finish up with the Prune and Armagnac parfait … it is to die for.

Owners	Marguerite Howley
Address	St. John's Point, Dunkineely, Co. Donegal.
Tel	074 9737022
No. Of Rooms	10
Price	
Double	From €120
Twin	From €120
Single	€80
Family	From €160
Dinner	Yes - Restaurant
Open	Mid February – Mid January. Closed Monday low season.
	Open every day high season.
Credit Cards	Visa MC Diners Amex
Directions	2 kms from Dunkineely Village
Email	info@castlemurray.com
Web	www.lucindaosullivan.com/castlemurray

Coxtown Manor

Some of the best restaurants in Europe are in Belgium but none of our M.E.P.s like to tell us this because they want us to think they are working so hard, travelling back and forth to Brussels. Certainly some of them seem to have added on a few kilos since they started the E.U.commute! One man who has come the other way and set up business in the north West, just outside Donegal Town and close to Donegal Bay, is Eduard Dewael with his fabulous late Georgian House, Coxtown Manor. The location is magnificent, the house is magnificent, the food is magnificent and service and attention are magnificent. I have not met anyone yet who has but raved about Coxtown Manor and this is a place we are going to be hearing a lot more of. The décor is very much of today, stripped floorboards, pretty colours and lovely furniture, adding a continental twist to his striking house. They have a wood panelled bar where you can try out some of the famous Belgian Strong Beers, Duval, Westmalle along with all the customary drinks. Dinner in the Restaurant offers a combination of Belgian/ Irish food or, I suppose you might say, the best of Irish produce cooked with a Belgian slant by Head Chef, Michel Aerts. Their fillet steaks are from the finest locally raised Charolais herds, the lamb is raised on Coxtown grounds, and with the Atlantic Ocean on their doorstep, believe me the fish is good. Eduard uses

free-range eggs, organic red label chicken – nothing but the best of produce. You will die for the famous Belgian chocolate desserts which feature largely on their repertoire. If you are a golfer, you have Donegal, Bundoran and Rosses Point Golf Courses from which to choose. Do a Hercule Poirot and come and investigate their Gourmet Weekends … you won't be disappointed. Oh just think, hot chocolate with a splash of Grand Marnier before you toddle up to bed … oh maybe I'll have another one!

Owners	Eduard Dewael
Address	Laghey, Co. Donegal.
Tel	0749734575
No. Of Rooms	10
Price	
Double/Twin	€150 - €210 B & B
	€238 - €298 B & B inc a la Carte Dinner for 2
Dinner	Yes
Open	All Year except 3 weeks November and 3 weeks January.
Credit Cards	Visa MC
Directions	Watch for sign on N15 between Ballycastle and Donegal Town.
Email	coxtownmanor@oddpost.com
Web	www.lucindaosullivan.com/coxtownmanor

 NET P

Donegal Manor

The mere mention of Donegal Town leads my husband into a reverie of remeniscences about his time spent there in the days of his childhood. He talks of Dan McBrearty's forge where he spent many an hour pumping the bellows.

He mentions the central Diamond, the O'Donnell Castle on the bank of the river Eske, and the particularly lovely "Church of the Four Masters" where women prayed on one side of the central aisle, and men on the other. That was all in the 40's and 50's and, like all over the country, things have changed.

Donegal Town is a very busy commercial centre, and probably one of the most friendly and welcoming places in the country, gateway to many places of historical and current interest in the county, and now boasts the exceptional Donegal Manor. This is not your run of the mill B & B but one of the new breed of boutique guest house accommodations.

The Manor, which was custom built in 2004, is run by Sian and Michael Breslin who fall over backwards to make your stay pleasant and enjoyable. All the bedrooms are spacious and are furnished to the highest possible standard with ensuite facilities. There is interesting original artwork on the walls, and very welcoming turf fires. Oh how I love the smell of burning turf

and there is Nana Murphy's tearooms too to supply needed sustenance all day. Each bedroom is also provided with a refreshment tray, TV, and for the business person there is Broadband connection in each room. The Manor also boasts a business centre where you can fax, print, scan, or copy documents at reasonable rates.

Donegal Manor is also more than family friendly. Children sharing with parents are free up to age 12 and, from 13- 18 years, they enjoy free accommodation (sharing room with parent) and just pay for breakfast. Breakfasts are excellent with each morning a fruit dish, maybe rhubarb and raspberry compote, apricots and prunes poached in a spicey juice, fresh fruit salad in summer, all served with Greek yoghurt. Their coarse brown bread is superb and they also do a super Porter Cake. Their local prize winning butcher supplies great sausages for the Full Irish … you won't go wrong at Donegal Manor – it is a place with a warm Donegal heart and great value.

Owners	Sian and Michael Breslin
Address	Letterkenny Road, Donegal Town, Co. Donegal.
Tel	074 9725222
No of Rooms	9
Price	
Double/twin	€90 - €110
Single	€55 - €70
Family	0-12 Stay Free BB. 13- 18 years free accomm sharing room with parents. Breakfast €10
Dinner	No
Open	1st March – 2nd January
Credit Cards	Yes
Directions	At 1st roundabout for Donegal Town, take 2nd exit onto bypass. At 2nd Roundabout, take last exit. Continue on N15, and take 2nd round to right.
Email	info@donegalmanor.com
Web	

www.lucindaosullivan.com/donegalmanor

Frewin

RAMELTON

Ramelton is an old plantation town with beautiful Georgian buildings sited on the River Lennan that flows into Lough Swilly. In times past the river was navigable by ocean going vessels and Ramelton was an important town for trade. The town itself was prosperous and homes were furnished with many exotic imported items. The Fishhouse, on the Quayside, has a town map listing a number of important buildings worth seeing. Eateries are plentiful and superb fresh fish is widely available.

FREWIN

Whether in winter or summer, Thomas and Regina Coyle's picture postcard pretty former rectory, Frewin, is a magnificent place to visit. Everything about the house, bedrooms, suites, and gardens, have been lovingly restored by the owners. Thomas hails from the area and has a knowledge of the countryside which would enthrall and keep visitors listening to local folklore for many an hour. Many of the bedrooms are decorated in white, with white painted furniture, and white muslin curtains. One of the bedrooms is just perfect for honeymooners or a romantic stay, a bridal suite complete with lace drapes over the bed, delicately carved mirrors, and beautiful ornaments adorn the room. Throughout, the house has retained its original character but with all modern facilites of course. Thomas and Regina have a great interest in antiques and restoration and there is a little antique shop and self catering cottage in the the grounds. The gardens are beautiful. Dinner is available with advance notice and you can bring your own wine if you wish. The diningroom is special, no electric lighting, but a really splendid atmosphere under a real candle lit chandelier.

You can relax after dinner in the lovely library. Thomas and Regina are warm and entertaining hosts who genuinely enjoy meeting their guests. Frewin is a place one doesn't want to leave. The house is not suitable for young children.

Owners	Thomas and Regina Coyle
Address	Ramelton, Co. Donegal.
Tel	074 9151246
No of Rooms	4 (3 en suite)
Price	
Double	€120 - €180
Twin	€170-€180
Single	€75 - €90
1 bed self catering cottage	€450-€550 per week
Dinner	Yes – Enquire on booking
Open	All year save Christmas
Credit Cards	Yes
Directions	Turn right at speed limits to Ramelton (coming from Letterkenny). Frewen 300 metres on right.
Email	flaxmill@indigo.ie
Web	

wwww.lucindaosullivan.com/frewin

 P

Harvey's Point Country Hotel

I n 1983 whilst on holidays from Switzerland, Jody Gysling, attracted by the stunning Swiss like snow capped Blue Stack Mountains, bought an old cottage on a swamp on the shores of Lough Eske, from two brothers by the name of Harvey. Jody gradually renovated the cottage, painstakingly drawing stones by tractor ten miles in the process. Six years later, escaping the pressures of Swiss business life, Jody and his brother Marc opened a small Guest House. A young local girl, Deirdre, took a summer job with them, romance blossomed between Deirdre and Marc and the rest, as they say, is history.

2004 was the turning point with major development and investment in Harvey's Point and what was once a tiny cottage is now a fabulous destination Hotel, nestling on the shores of shimmering Lough Eske 42 fab new bedrooms and suites were added in keeping with the beauty and integrity of the area. From traditional Swiss designs, the bright airy rooms feature classically comfortable wooden furniture complimented with every conceivable modern convenience. There are four categories of accommodation from which to choose, each absolutely fantastic with amazing facilities. Executive rooms have a separate foyer, kingsize beds, mini bars, Broadband Internet access. De Luxe rooms are a larger version of the Executive category. Premium suites offer all of the above along with a private dressing room, whirlpool baths and lake views and then you have the fab

Penthouse Suites double the size of the Executive Suites with bedroom, living room, bar area, lounge, dressing room, guest wc, whirlpool and bath, king size bed. Latest additions to the luxury of Harvey's Point include new Beauty Treatment and Hairdressings Facilities as well as a new Boardroom with a capacity of 25 for corporate groups.

Food too is a major feature at Harvey's Point. The restaurant sweeps down to the water and there is a French slant to the delicious cuisine - Donegal Bay oysters or maybe a terrine of duck foie gras flavoured with Irish Mist liqueur whilst shellfish and prawn bisque comes with a puff pastry lid. Follow up then maybe with black sole or duo of Donegal lamb, scallops or monkfish but leave room for the luscious puds.

The scenery is spectacular in Donegal and the friendliness of the people well known whether you land on the helicopter pad or by car – get yourself to Harvey's Point – it is different and it is beautiful.

Owners	Deirdre McGlone & Marc Gysling
Address	Lough Eske, Donegal Town, Co. Donegal.
Tel	074 9722208
No. Of Rooms	62
Price	
Double/Twin	€290
Single	€240
Dinner	Yes
Open	All Year (Nov – March closed Sun/Mon/Tues nights)
Credit Cards	All Major Cards
Directions	6km from Donegal Town. Follow signs for Lough Eske.
Email:	info@harveyspoint.com
Web:	
www.lucindaosullivan.com/harveyspoint	

NET H P

The Sandhouse Hotel &
Marine Spa

ust off the main road, between Bundoran and Donegal Town, is the magnificent sweeping beach at Rosnowlagh, on the Atlantic Coast of Donegal, where stands the lovely Sandhouse Hotel and Marine Spa. Virtually on the beach, you simply could not get any closer to sun, sea and sand!

Originally a Fishing Lodge it was transformed by the Britton family into the fine hotel it is today. Most of its bedrooms, furnished in lavish country house style, have spectacular views over Donegal Bay and its proximity to the Ocean, and its food, have always been star points. Seafood is a speciality at the aptly named Seashell Restaurant and oysters, crab, scallops, lobster, sourced from local unpolluted waters, are regularly on the menu, as well as delicious Donegal lamb, prime beef and veal, and game in season. During the day locally smoked salmon, fresh Donegal Bay oysters and mussels are also served in the cosy bar

I think we've come to realise how important it is to be able to switch off, walk the beach, and take the sea air. The Victorians used to take the waters and visit Spa towns, as did the Germans and Austrians, and way back the Romans. We are now only realising, but realising in a big way, how important water therapy is. At the Spa Suite at the Sandhouse they offer the very best in Marine

Body and Skin Care with Thalgo Marine, which uses 100% pure seaweed from the coast of Northern France. The richness of the sea oligo elements, proteins, amino acids and vitamins are captured within the Thalgo philosophy and are vital to health and well being, and ensure soft supple revitalised skin. Try the Balneotherapy, a high-powered bath with 200 water jets massaging all those tender spots like lower back and neck. Think of it, aromatic oils, mineral salts, dried seaweed. Sure, after all that toning and rejuvenation you will be running up and down the beach every day, and knocking back the champagne in the bar each evening.

Apart from walking, surfing or just relaxing the Sandhouse is within easy reach of many championship standard golf courses and Rosnowlagh is an ideal centre from which to explore places of historical and cultural interest.

The Sandhouse Hotel is one of those great places to which you feel you are coming home each time you arrive. Feel the sand between your toes.

Owners	The Britton Family
	Paul Diver - Manager
Address	Rossnowlagh Beach, Rossnowlagh, Donegal Bay,
	Co. Donegal.
Tel	071 9851777
No. Of Rooms	55
Price	
Double/Twin	€200
Single	€100
Family	€100 per adult with reductions for children
Dinner	Yes
Open	February - December
Credit Cards	All Major Cards
Directions	From Ballyshannon take the Coast Road to Rossnowlagh.
Email	info@sandhouse.ie
Web	www.lucindaosullivan.com/sandhouse

County Dublin

ounty Dublin is dominated by Ireland's Capital City, Dublin. The city exudes the style and confidence of any European Capital but its citizens still know how to party and enjoy themselves like there was no tomorrow. Set on the fine sweep of Dublin Bay, the city is divided by the River Liffey, which flows from west to east. South of the river are the fine examples of Dublin's Georgian past with the lovely Fitzwilliam and Merrion Squares, and the beautiful St. Stephen's Green with its rich and colourful flowerbeds, green lawns, dreamy ponds and shaded walkways. North of the river is the Municipal Art Gallery, the Writers Museum, as well as the Phoenix Park, one of the largest enclosed parks in the world and the residence of the Country's President and the U.S. Ambassador – a favourite haunt of Dubliners. The city abounds with places and buildings that remind us of Ireland's historic and troubled past. The General Post Office was the scene of violent fighting in 1916. Dublin Castle was seat of the British Occupation Control, and Kilmainham Jail has many shadows of the past. Round the Bay to the South the road leads through fashionable Monkstown with its crescent of lively restaurants, on to the town of Dun Laoire with its harbour and yacht clubs, to Sandycove and its association with James Joyce. Further South is the magnificent sweep of Killiney Beach and the homes of many rich and famous. North of the city are some lovely and friendly seaside towns and villages – the very fashionable Malahide, the busy fishing town of Howth, the fine sandy beach of Portmarnock with its famous Golf Links and Skerries, a favourite spot for Dubliners and visitors alike. As the song says … Dublin can be Heaven.

"Other people have a nationality, the Irish and the Jews have a psychosis"

(Brendan Behan)

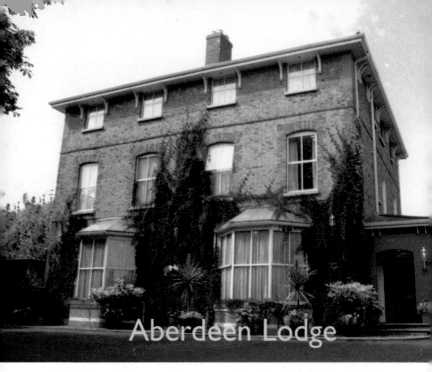

Aberdeen Lodge

You won't find any "Basil Fawlty's" at Pat Halpin's Aberdeen Lodge, in the heart of Dublin's leafy embassy belt, Ballsbridge. Pat, the ultimate Hotelier, quietly misses nothing, is supremely helpful and efficient whilst, seemingly effortlessly, running four small private Hotels. Nothing is too much trouble for the staff at Aberdeen who are motivated to provide the 5 star standard of friendliness and helpfulness expected by the Head Man. Aberdeen Lodge is a large Edwardian Villa on its own grounds expertly converted to provide accommodation of the very highest standard. Fine bedrooms, some with four-posters and whirpool spa baths, have Satellite T.V. Mineral Water, trouser press, all the little details. There is an elegant drawingroom with plenty to read and you can order from their substantial Drawingroom and Room Service Menu. They also have a wine list. Breakfast is brilliant – a lavish buffet displayed in pretty Nicholas Mosse pottery followed by a hot selection. Breakfast is included in the room rate but if you want to have a business meeting over breakfast you can invite a guest to join you. There is also complimentary wireless Internet access for guests. Ballsbridge is where the Royal Dublin Society have their magnificent Showgrounds and is the venue of the famous Dublin Horse Show. Down the road is Lansdowne Road – the headquarters of Irish rugby. If you are a resident and your address is "Dublin 4" that says it all about you – money – class - although nowadays there is a fair scattering of nouveaux Celtic Tiger money types infiltrating the red bricked roads. Location, location, location is the story at Ballsbridge, for you can walk into the centre of Town in 15 minutes, the DART station is nearby at Sydney Parade or taxis will be

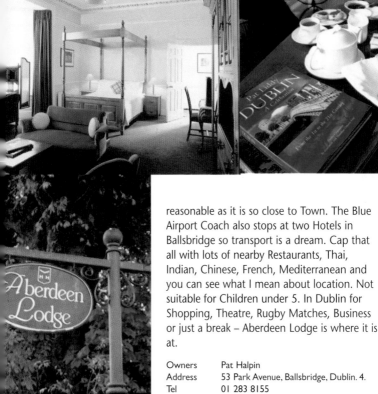

reasonable as it is so close to Town. The Blue Airport Coach also stops at two Hotels in Ballsbridge so transport is a dream. Cap that all with lots of nearby Restaurants, Thai, Indian, Chinese, French, Mediterranean and you can see what I mean about location. Not suitable for Children under 5. In Dublin for Shopping, Theatre, Rugby Matches, Business or just a break – Aberdeen Lodge is where it is at.

Owners	Pat Halpin
Address	53 Park Avenue, Ballsbridge, Dublin. 4.
Tel	01 283 8155
No. Of Rooms	19
Price	
Suite	€225 - €295
Double/Twin	€140 - €170
Family	€160 - €190
Single	€90 - €129
Dinner	Drawingroom Menu
Open	All Year
Credit Cards	Visa MC Amex Diners
Directions	Down the road from Sydney Parade DART Station. Park Avenue runs parallel with Merrion Road and Strand Road close to RDS.
Email	aberdeen@iol.ie
Web:	www.lucindaosullivan.com/aberdeenlodge

Conrad Hotel Dublin

There was a time in Dublin when the Hotels in which to be seen were the old Hibernian Hotel on Dawson Street way back before my time, the Russell Hotel on St Stephen's Green long since gone.

Those were the days of big Hollywood stars. We had all heard of Elizabeth Taylor being married at 18 to Hotel magnate Conrad Hilton's son, Nicky, just as we hear talk today of Paris Hilton, so there was a great air of excitement and whiff of glamour in Dublin when the Conrad Dublin opened in 1989. It was the first international Hotel to have opened in the City in 30 years and was an immediate success.

Superbly located on Earlsfort Terrace, just off St. Stephen's Green, facing the National Concert Hall, the 5 Star Conrad Dublin is just a few minutes walk from fashionable Grafton Street. It is also very convenient for the National Gallery, Trinity College, the National Museum and Georgian Dublin. I did an article not so long ago on Hotel Lobbies and the interesting people who frequented them for coffee or drinks and, in the Conrad, I nearly fell backwards trying to overhear the conversation between a well known Irish Builder and Politician. Unfortunately I will never know the outcome! So it is always worth keeping your eyes open in the Conrad because there are lots of famous people who've stayed there, including Billy Connolly, Mimi Rogers,

Rod Stewart and Senator Hilary Clinton.

A major refurbishment programme costing €15m has just been completed and the hotel now offers 192 spacious guest rooms along with 24-hour room service, a fitness centre and an underground car park. Their new urban cool Alex Restaurant and Bar specialises in really good seafood so you can indulge yourself in caviar or lobster, but do try the brown shrimp risotto which is sublime. A glass screen links the restaurant to the Cocktail Bar and, oh boy, can I testify to the fact that the cocktails are stunners! The Hotel also has a traditional Irish Pub, "Alfie Byrne's", named after a much loved former Lord Mayor and doing excellent pub food.

The level of service at the Conrad is amazing and, coupled with everything else I have told you, it is a really Great Place to Stay in Dublin, I love that frisson of glam…

Owners	Laurens Zieren (General Manager)
Address	Earlsfort Terrace, Dublin. 2.
Tel	01-602 8900
No. of Rooms	192
Price	
Double/Twin	€195-€285
Single	€195-€285
Dinner	Yes – Restaurant and Bar food
Open	All Year
Credit Cards	Visa MC Amex Diners Laser
Directions	From Dublin Airport, take the M1/N1 to the City Centre. Follow signs to St. Stephen's Green. Hotel located off St. Stephen's Green opposite National Concert Hall.

Email
dublininfo@conradhotels.com
Web:
www.lucindaosullivan.com/conradhotel

dylan
Hotel

"It was the White Rabbit, trotting slowly …looking anxiously… The Duchess! The Duchess! Oh my dear paws! Oh my fur and whiskers!" Maybe I did see the White Rabbit in the new "dylan Hotel" on Eastmoreland Place, or was I dreaming, for it is like waking up in Alice's Wonderland? Quite amazing.

The dylan is a hot new Boutique Hotel which hit the ground running. The décor is funky and wild and there is a London-ish feel to the little cul de sac where it is located. Just five minutes from St. Stephen's Green and Grafton Street, it is perfectly placed in the up market side of town. Outside is a lovely big terrace, which will be a social scene on balmy summer evenings. In the hallway is a padded purple button backed designer chair shaped like a languishing lady, just one of the many feature pieces throughout. The bar is a hive of activity doing great cocktails.

The bedrooms are stunning with fabulous French headboards, Frette bedlinen, magnificent drapes, lush brocade covered chairs, big plump pillows, plasma screen TV's and MP3 players, Internet access, mini bars and twice-daily housekeeping. The bathrooms are to die for with underfloor heating, Etro toiletries – just pure heaven – one room is more fabulous than the next.

Don't even think of going out to a restaurant before you have been to their Still Restaurant - which is like a Fairy Queen's Ice Palace – white white white. It only seats 44 people so book in advance. Down the centre of the room are 18 little crystal chandeliers, lots of silver gilt furnishings, great big White Queen's pearlised giant high backed thrones mixing with virtually backless chairs. Lots of white

button-backed leatherette banquette details, wild mirrors, crisp white napery and white porcelain.

The food is fabulous … serious food in frothy surroundings. We had Foie Gras served with confit pork belly on a cep puree with Puy lentil jus and Seared rare Blue Fin tuna with a citrus dressing, sorrel aioli and radish. To follow we had absolutely glorious roasted venison – three little towers on a root vegetable terrine, parsnip puree and black trompettes and exquisite turbot with a little pot of incredibly intense crab soufflé into which was poured prawn bisque. The puddings are out of this world so don't pass and, for wine buffs, the list is like a bible – but prices to suit all pockets.

A real wonderland.

Owner	Seamus Ross
Address	Eastmoreland Place, Dublin. 4.
Tel	01 6603000
No of Rooms	44
Price	
Double/twin	€395 - €440
Suites	€690 - €800
Dinner	Yes - Restaurant
Open	All Year - save 24th – 26th December
Credit Cards	Yes
Directions	From St. Stephen's Green, go down Baggot Street. Cross Grand Canal and take left after Searson's Pub on to Eastmoreland Place.
Email	justask@dylan.ie
Web	www.lucindaosullivan.com/dylanhotel

Hotel Isaacs

The owners of Hotel Isaacs showed great foresight in 1979 when they first opened up their Isaacs Hostel in the city centre for this was not even on the cusp of the Celtic Tiger boom. Eleven years ago they opened Hotel Isaacs, which at that stage had only 25 rooms, and they followed up the following year with their very successful Il Vignardo restaurant. Hotel Isaacs, which provides very good value hotel accommodation, right in the heart of the City, was so successful it just grew and grew. Close to the Financial Services Centre, the Central Bus Station, the DART, the LUAS, it is perfect for brilliant value city breaks. A short walk brings you to Trinity College, O'Connell Street, or if you go the other direction you can take in the concerts at the Point.

There are now 90 bedrooms designated 3 Star. All are very comfortably furnished, both standard and superior rooms. They have TV, tea and coffee making facilities, trouser press, iron and board, safe, room service, air conditioning in some, and the now de rigueur facility of WIFI Internet access, which is just brilliant.

However, ever on the upwards move, The Isaacs Group late last year bought No 2 Beresford Place, a wonderful Gandon designed Georgian House, which overlooks The Custom House – what a spectacular outlook. There are fourteen beautiful bedrooms in this glorious building which will serve, in conjunction with No. 1 Beresford Place, which is their meeting and conference centre, as their executive accommodation and conference wing. This magnificent house can also be rented for private and corporate parties and they will provide a delicious buffet menu which you can tailor to suit your own pocket and requirements.

Originally a wine warehouse, their light hearted and fun Restaurant Il Vignardo, which also has a courtyard

garden, is located in a beautiful Italianate room with marbled columns and curved vaulted style ceilings, doing popular Italian food - pastas, pizzas, chicken and beef dishes. They have a great early bird a la carte at €8.90 for any pizza or pasta dish. Try the Amatriciana with smoked bacon, onions, chili and tomato – yum. They also have Le Monde Café Bar which is a very attractive space too – reminiscent of a middle European brasserie – where they also do light lunches as well as specialty coffees and wines.

There are limited private parking spaces which must be pre-booked.

Owners	Justin Lowry (General Manager)
Address	Store Street, Dublin. 1.
Tel	Tel: 01 8134700
No of Rooms	104
Price	
Double/twin	€70 - €250
Single	€70 - €250
Family	€100 - €300
Dinner	Yes - Restaurant
Open	All Year save 23rd – 26th December
Credit Cards	Yes
Directions	Opposite Busaras and the Custom House
Email	hotel@isaacs.ie
Web	www.lucindaosullivan.com/hotelisaacs

The Merrion Hotel

During the 18th century, Dublin was transformed from a mediaeval town into one of the finest Georgian cities in Europe. The 5 Star Merrion Hotel, which opened in 1997, is set in the heart of Georgian Dublin, opposite Government Buildings and comprises four meticulously restored Grade 1 Georgian townhouses and a specially commissioned garden wing around private period gardens. Built in 1760 the most important of these houses is Mornington House, birthplace of the 1st Duke of Wellington. Quite magnificently structured, the doors, architraves, the intricate delicate fanlights, heavy staircases, and amazing rococo plasterwork are just a pleasure to absorb

Dubliners have clasped The Merrion to their bosom for a splendidly gracious atmosphere has been maintained whilst being elegantly unstuffy. The interior is designed using Irish fabrics and antiques reflecting the original interiors. The public rooms are welcoming and serene – particularly the Drawingrooms and terrace - where one can sit and have afternoon tea or a drink in the most civilized of surroundings, whilst also enjoying one of the finest private collections of 19th and 20th century Art for works by Mary Swanzy, Roderic O'Conor, Sir John Lavery, Paul Henry, and many more, are set against this beautiful backdrop.

100

There are two in-house restaurants - Patrick Guilbaud's, the superb 2 Michelin starred establishment and the beautiful Cellar Restaurant, with its cool uplit vault style columns and pale tiled floor. Here too the food is sublime and very reasonably priced apart at all from the fact that you are sitting in one of the finest 5 star hotels in Ireland.

The restoration of The Merrion demanded the highest standards and the designers' brief was both simple and clear – "To create a space with sensitivity to the 18th century heritage of the building with light and airy bedrooms". As a result, the guest rooms and suites are the epitome of elegance and also supremely inviting and comfortable, not to mention the most spectacular Penthouse Suite in Dublin.

There is also the beautiful Tethra Spa which offers a comprehensive choice of bodycare and beauty treatments using exclusive E'SPA products so this is just the place to relax after a hard day shopping in nearby Grafton Street or visiting the National Gallery and Museums just across the way.

The Merrion Hotel is Heaven on Earth – nothing more, nothing less.

Owners	Peter McCann
	General Manager
Address	Upper Merrion Street,
	Dublin 2.
Tel	01-6030600
No. Of Rooms	143
Price	
Double/Twin	From €470
Single	From €450
Dinner	Yes – 2 Restaurants
Open	All Year
Credit Cards	All Major Credit Cards
Directions	From the top of Grafton Street, turn left, continue on straight and take the third turn left on to Upper Merrion Street.
Email:	info@merrionhotel.com
Web:	
www.lucindaosullivan.com/merrionhotel	

Spa | NET | P

Redbank House and Restaurant

SKERRIES, CO. DUBLIN.

Skerries is a fishing village north of Dublin which is forever in my heart as I spent summers there as a child. It all now seems so simple and real. We would swim on the sandy shore of the south beach be it rain or shine. I still remember being enveloped in a big soft towel and dried off on a wet day whilst the aroma of the frying chips and salt were blown down the beach. My mother would buy prawns from the fishermen while my father slipped into the Stoop Your Head or Joe May's for a pint and a half one, which is the colloquialism for a Pint of Guinness and a whiskey. Daddy would then have a smile on his chops as Mother and I would drop the live prawns into the boiling pot for a whisker of a second, take them out and eat them with salt. The local Cinema heralded the delights of Lilac Time with Anna Neagle warbling "we'll gather lilacs in the spring again" ... it was a hundred years old then and it seems like a thousand years old now ... but Skerries at its heart still retains a wonderful untouched sense of the real Ireland for it is largely undiscovered by tourists.

REDBANK HOUSE AND RESTAURANT

The Redbank House and Restaurant is owned and run by one of Ireland's best-known Chefs, Terry McCoy. Terry is a familiar figure on the Irish foodie scene, not just because he is a striking figure who sports a ponytail and beard but because he wins awards all round him for his handling of very fine

seafood caught off the Fingal coast. Whilst the Red Bank Restaurant has been a destination Restaurant for the past 20 years or so it is only in the past couple of years that Terry added 18 rooms by way of the Old Bank House beside the Restaurant and nearby The Red Bank Lodge. The rooms are comfortably furnished with all mod cons and comforts in cool nautical colours, blues, yellows and cream, but with a warmth of feeling. All have T.V. and Internet access. This is a house too for the Gourmet Golfer, for there are forty golf courses within "a driver and a sand wedge" of Skerries and what is better after a quick one at the 19th hole than to come back to enjoy Terry's hospitality and fabulous treatment of our wonderful Dublin Bay Prawns and other seafood. Try the Razor fish, caught locally, which are mainly exported to Japan and also ask the see the wine cellar in the old Bank Vault. The Red Bank's long Sunday lunches are legendary. St. Patrick who drove the snakes out of Ireland lived on Church Island off Skerries and fed himself on goat's milk and goats cheese so you see chevre was popular in Skerries before anywhere else in Ireland! Skerries is only 18 miles from Dublin, easily commutable by train, and is only 20 minutes drive from Dublin Airport. Walk the beaches; feel the sea breeze in your hair and the sand between your toes, chill out, it is the place.

Owners	Terry McCoy
Address	5-7 Church Street, Skerries, Co. Dublin.
Tel	01 849 1005
No. Of Rooms	18
Price	
Double/Twin	€120
Single	€75
Family	€120 + €25 per extra person including breakfast
Dinner	Yes - Restaurant
Open	All Year – Restaurant closed for dinner Sunday nights, and also 24th, 25th and 26th December.
Credit Cards	All major cards
Directions	Opposite AIB Skerries
Email	info@redbank.ie
Web	www.lucindaosullivan.com/redbankhouse

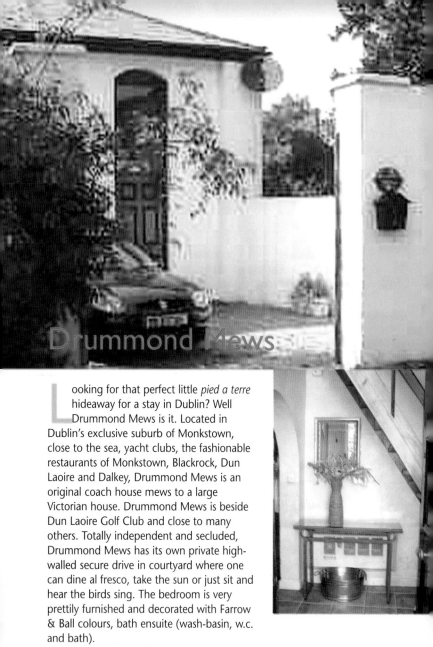

Drummond Mews

Looking for that perfect little *pied a terre* hideaway for a stay in Dublin? Well Drummond Mews is it. Located in Dublin's exclusive suburb of Monkstown, close to the sea, yacht clubs, the fashionable restaurants of Monkstown, Blackrock, Dun Laoire and Dalkey, Drummond Mews is an original coach house mews to a large Victorian house. Drummond Mews is beside Dun Laoire Golf Club and close to many others. Totally independent and secluded, Drummond Mews has its own private high-walled secure drive in courtyard where one can dine al fresco, take the sun or just sit and hear the birds sing. The bedroom is very prettily furnished and decorated with Farrow & Ball colours, bath ensuite (wash-basin, w.c. and bath).

Downstairs has a large Mediterranean style tiled living cum dining area with small but more than pleasing galley kitchen, fully equipped with microwave, washer-dryer. There is also satellite T.V. and all bed linen and towels are supplied free of charge.

Dublin Tourism 3 Star graded. 10 minutes walk to the DART station,

which whisks you into central Dublin in 15 minutes and the 46A bus runs from the top of the road serving U.C.D. Drummond Mews is also very convenient for the Sandyford/Stillorgan Estate for people on temporary assignments to Dublin and has easy access to the M50.

Owners	Mary O'Sullivan
Address	Monkstown, Co. Dublin
Tel/Fax	01 2800419
No. Of Rooms	Mews House sleeps 2
Price	€695 per week
Dinner	Self Catering
Open	All Year
Credit Cards	Visa MC
Directions	Phone above

Email	info@dublin-accommodation.net
Web	www.lucindaosullivan.com/drummondmews

County Galway

As a county, Galway encompasses a University City, the wild splendour and magnificence of Connemara and the Twelve Bens then, to cap it all, you have the Aran Islands. Galway City has a vibrancy all of its own and straddles the Corrib river which thunders down under the Salmon Weir Bridge and winds itself around the City to the lively pedestrianised Quay Street at Wolfe Tone Bridge, where the river enters the famous Galway Bay. Worth seeing is the Spanish Arch, a 16th century structure used to protect galleons unloading wine and rum – most important - and the Collegiate Church of St. Nicholas of Myra, the largest mediaeval church in Ireland, built in 1320 dedicated to the patron saint of sailors. It is almost impossible to find a bed in Galway during Race Week, the Arts Festival, and the Oyster Festival at Clarinbridge so book early. The City abounds with Art Galleries and here you can also visit the home of Nora Barnacle, wife of James Joyce, which is now a small museum. Beyond the Claddagh village from which originated the Claddagh ring – is Salthill – the more honky tonk holiday area with amusement arcades. Moving west around the coast road you come to An Spideal or Spiddle, the heart of the Gaeltacht. Inland is Oughterard, a long pretty village on the River Owenriff, which is very popular with anglers. Oughterard is the gateway to Connemara but a

wonderful base for a holiday or break for those who want to have easy access to Galway City. Clifden is the capital of Connemara and is laid out in a triangle. Small and compact but with wide streets and buildings perched high above the deep estuary of the River Owenglin, Clifden is renowned for its Connemara Pony Show. Many famous Irish artists, Paul Henry, Maurice MacGonigal, Jack Yeats, and Sean Keating, have immortalized Clifden in their paintings. The Alcock & Brown Memorial, which commemorates the first transatlantic flight in 1919, is worth seeing. Ten miles northeast of Clifden is Letterfrack, a 19th century Quaker village and just

northwest of that is the magnificent Renvyle peninsula, which has strong literary associations.

"A good holiday is one spent among people whose notions of time
are vaguer than yours"
(J.B. Priestly)

Galway Radisson SAS Hotel and Spa

The Galway Radisson SAS Hotel and Spa is to the Hotel Industry what the Lamborghini is to the Motor biz! Sleek in design, powerful in body, the Galway Radisson just purrs. Established in 2001, this 4 Star hotel is only five minutes walk from Eyre Square but boasts fabulous views of Lough Atalia and Galway Bay. The magnificent glass Atrium of the hotel's foyer sets the scene of lightness and clarity within. The stylish Atrium Bar and Lounge with tinkling piano opens out onto a heated terrace where you can have a drink and watch "the sun go down on Galway Bay". The rooms are pretty fab – 217 in total in various categories and with three room styles: Maritime, Scandinavian, or Classic. There are Standard, Superior, Business Class, Junior Suites, Executive Suites and Rooms catering for people with a disability. All rooms have a Power Tower, a space saving device that offers satellite television with movie channels, coffee/tea-maker, minibar, personal safe......... whilst the Executive Suites represent the world's highest technological standards. If you really want to splash out Level 5 is top drawer - where Guests are guaranteed privacy and personal service in 16 spacious luxurious executive rooms. Included in Level 5 is a Club Lounge, complimentary treats served throughout the day, soft drinks and canapés during Club Hour, secure membership only access, panoramic rooftop terrace, free use of the Business Service Centre and a separate meeting room... The stylish split level 220 seater Restaurant Marina is a vision of blue, integrated with dark walnut, reflecting the nautical theme and, as Galway is famous for its seafood, that is the specialty - Galway Bay Oysters, Scallops, Lobster, Monkfish – but there are delicious carnivorous options too. Chill out in the Spirit One Spa with facilities found only in the best destination Spas in the world - Sabia Med, Hammam, Rocksauna, Aroma Grotto, Tropical Rain

Shower, Cold Fog Showers, Ice Drench and Heated Loungers. The Leisure Centre's Swimming Pool is fab along with children's Pool, Jacuzzi, Sauna, Outdoor Canadian Hot Tub.

How could you beat that - Radisson Galway is fantastic.

Owners	Tom Flanagan
(General Manager)	
Address	Lough Atalia Road, Galway.
Tel	091 538300
No. Of Rooms	217
Price	
Penthouse	€1500
Suites Level 5	€299
Double/Twin	€240
Single	€220
Family	€270
Dinner	Yes
Open	All Year
Credit Cards	All Major Cards
Directions	5 minutes from Eyre Square on Lough Atalia waterfront.

Email:	reservations.galway@radissonsas.com
Web:	www.lucindaosullivan.com/radissongalway

Renvyle House Hotel

"My house … stands on a lake, but it stands also on the sea – waterlillies meet the golden seaweed. It is as if, in the faery land of Connemara at the extreme end of Europe, the incongruous flowed together at last, and the sweet and bitter blended. Behind me, islands and mountainous mainland share in a final reconciliation, at this, the world's end." So wrote Oliver St. John Gogarty in 1927 of his then home. Spectacularly located nestling between the blue Twelve Bens mountain range and the Shores of the Atlantic Ocean, Renvyle has a tremendous history and it has always attracted famous people from all over the world. The house has been pulled down, rebuilt, burnt to ashes, rebuilt again. It has been home to Donal O'Flaherty, Chieftan of  one of the oldest and most powerful Clans of Connaught, and to Mrs. Caroline Blake who was the first to open it as a hotel way back in 1883. But, enough of the past, for Renvyle has been a hotel for all seasons and has always moved with the times and is a stylish destination which is hugely popular with the Irish public, who return again and again for blissful respite and evenings filled with fun. Situated on a 200 acre Estate, Renvyle has a lake teaming with trout, a heated outdoor pool, a new-improved 9-hole links golf course and its own beach. There is clay pigeon shooting, horse riding in season, and buckets of activities and creche facilities during holiday periods. Pets are allowed "within reason" – enquire – for that doesn't mean Pooch can sit up with his Cartier collar at the dining table! Throughout the year there are Painting Breaks, Murder Mystery Weekends, Fly Fishing instruction, Golf Breaks and Walking Breaks. Sixty- eight bedrooms and five suites, are spacious and very comfortable with all that even the most difficult guest could possibly desire. Excellent food is based on fresh local produce,

Connemara lamb, game, fresh fish. In fact Renvyle Chef, Tim O'Sullivan, is a winner of the Moreau Chablis fish cookery competition. Classical Pianist, Derek Hoffman, accompanies dinner each evening, on Count John McCormack's Steinway Grand Piano – playing it that is! Oh, I want to get in the car and drive there again this minute … Ronnie Counihan runs a great house…

Owner:	John Coyle
Chief Executive	Ronnie Counihan
Address:	Renvyle, Connemara, Co. Galway.
Tel	095 43511
No. Of Rooms	68
Price	
Double/Twin	€80 - €230
Single	€40 - €115
Family	€110 - €345 (2 Adults + 2 Children)
Dinner	Yes - Restaurant
Open	February – January
Credit Cards	All Major Cards
Directions	Take N59 from Galway to Renvyle. Hotel signposted in village.
Email	info@renvyle.com
Web	www.lucindaosullivan.com

      NET H P

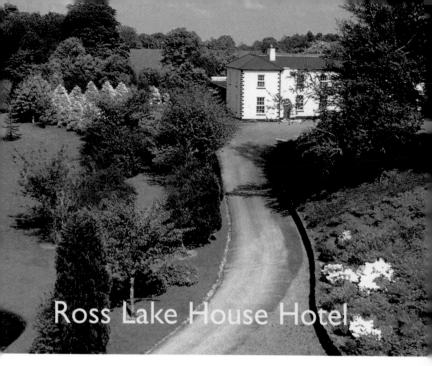

Ross Lake House Hotel

Fancy waking up in a four-poster bed in a splendid Georgian house, on 6 acres of rambling woods and rolling lawns, in the magnificent wilderness of Connemara, then Henry and Elaine Reid's Ross Lake House Hotel is for you. Ross Lake House was formerly part of the Killaguile estate built by James Edward Jackson, land agent for Lord Iveagh at Ashford Castle, but renamed as a Country House Hotel because of its proximity to Ross Lake and the fishing waters of Lough Corrib. With 13 spacious guestrooms and suites, all beautifully and individually designed to reflect the charm and graciousness of the house, yet provide the modern facilities we all expect nowadays, you will be very comfortable. There are lovely classic rooms oozing with country house charm, fabulous superior rooms with period furniture and luxurious fabrics, and then, stunning suites with their own sitting area. As pretty Oughterard is only 22 km from Galway City it is ideal for visiting the vibrancy that is Galway, but choosing to leave it when you wish. There are Golf Courses all round –

Oughterard, Barna, Galway Bay and Ballyconneely Links Course so if he wants to swing a club you can take off to the Antique shops. You are also ideally poised at Ross Lake for doing the rugged wilder aspects of the Connemara of "The Quiet Man". There is a cosy library bar to snuggle into and an elegant drawingroom with blazing fires to retire to after dinner and make new friends over a nightcap of the liquid variety. The dining room is gracious and the Chef concentrates on the finest fresh produce from the Connemara hills, rivers, lakes and the Atlantic Ocean so you can expect beautiful crabmeat, wild salmon, tender lamb, scrumptious desserts and fine wines.

Henry and Elaine are charming and helpful hosts and, believe me, you will really enjoy a spell at their lovely Ross Lake House.

Owners	Henry and Elaine Reid
Address	Rosscahill, Oughterard, Co. Galway.
Tel	091 550109
No. Of Rooms	13
Price	
Double/Twin	€150 - €170
Single	€105 - €115
Family	€190 - €220
Dinner	Yes
Open	March 15 to October 31st
Credit Cards	All Major Cards
Directions	Follow N59 towards Clifden. Hotel signposted after Moycullen.
Email	rosslake@iol.ie
Web	www.lucindaosullivan.com/rosslakehousehotel

County Kerry

Co. Kerry is known as "the Kingdom" and it is difficult to know where one starts to list the attractions of this amazing area. There is the world famous Killarney with its three lakes and impressive McGillycuddy Reeks looming behind them with their ever changing shades and colours. Almost as well known is the hair raising and breathtaking Ring of Kerry on the Iveragh peninsula with its sheer drops and stark coastal scenery. Coaches are required to travel anti-clockwise and leave Killarney between 10 and 11 a.m. so if you are doing it in a day, you need to be earlier or you will be behind them all day.

Some books tell you to drive clockwise but it can be nerve racking if you meet a coach on a narrow pass as I have experienced. Head out to Killorglin famous for its mid-August Puck Fair where eating, drinking, dancing, singing is reigned over by the King of the Festival, a Puck Goat. From Killorglin move on taking in the beautiful Caragh Lake to

"A folk song is a song nobody ever wrote" (anon)

Glenbeigh with Rossbeigh's sweeping beach. On to Cahersiveen and swing out via the new bridge to Valentia island. Come back and head south to Waterville where Charlie Chaplin and family spent their summers. The final stage is Caherdaniel to Sneem and the lush subtropical richness of Parknasilla which is then about eighteen miles from the popular town of Kenmare. North of the county is Listowel famous for its Writers Week and generally regarded as the literary capital of Ireland but also celebrates a madly popular Horse Race Week. Tralee, the principal town of the county, is a very busy commercial centre and also hosts the famous Rose of Tralee celebration. Dingle of "Ryan's Daughter" fame is stunning and has a life of its own. It also

has Fungi the dolphin. Among Kerry's many famous Championship Golf Courses is Ballybunion, the favourite haunt of American golfer, Tom Watson, who was once captain of the famous Club. Kerry has an abundance of eateries at all prices and in keeping with Irish tradition is well catered for in drinking establishments, many of which provide ballads and folk songs.

Aghadoe Heights Hotel & Spa

Aghadoe Heights Hotel at Killarney is not just any ordinary Hotel, it is a unique experience. 5 star unpretentious luxury at your fingertips, just the right distance outside the centre of the Town, directly overlooking the Killarney Lakes. The Aghadoe Heights is bliss and switch off time, from which you will only be disturbed by the solicitous and gentle pampering of the ever-attentive staff – they are fantastic – all of your whims just seem to be your pleasure. The public rooms are furnished with a mélange of elegant eclectic pieces from the Far East, mixed through with French antiques, a fine modern Irish art collection, and sculptures. Luxurious elegant bedrooms have balconies, whilst spacious junior suites with floor to ceiling windows have fantastic quadraphonic high tech TV's as well. A Roman style indoor swimming pool is placed to the front of the building so, as you swim, you can still see the lakes and mountains with their ever changing palette of moody colours. Right next door to the pool is a new hip cocktail bar for that cool drink or you can slip upstairs to the open plan lounge and have the most scrumptious afternoon tea, served by white gloved girls. Luxuriate in the fantastic new Aveda Spa. Try the Precious Stone Therapy – Aghadoe have the only Precious Stone Room in the world where you sit on a throne facing an amethyst grotto, it is blissful. In the evening you will be relaxed and ready for delicious

food in Frederick's Restaurant, which is incorporated in the large first floor open plan area, where the resident pianist plays away on the grand piano. They have their own lobster tank or you might fancy the best sole on the bone, or Oysters Rockefeller, or smoked fillet of venison with fresh linguine, juniper and orange jus … To cap it all Aghadoe now has the most fantastic two bedroomed penthouse suite, with outdoor hot tub, exquisitely furnished to include pieces by style icon Eileen Gray, as well as paintings by Maria Simmonds Gooding, and Pat Scott, and it has its own Paul Burrell – a butler who won't tell all! Chauffeur service to and from Kerry Airport available or come by helicopter. "How can you buy Killarney" were the words of the song but how can you buy Aghadoe is the real question!

Owners:	Pat & Marie Chawke
	(General Managers)
Address	Aghadoe, Lakes of Killarney, Co. Kerry.
Tel	064 31766
No. Of Rooms	97
Price	
Penthouse	€2,500
Double/Twin	€210 - €650
Single	Rack Rate + €65
Family	Rack Rate + €50 per child per night
	(max 2 Children under 16)
Dinner	Yes - Restaurant
Open	Mid March - End December
Credit Cards	All Major Cards
Directions	2 miles west of Killarney, signposted off N22

Email:	info@aghadoeheights.com
Web:	
www.lucindaosullivan.com/aghadoeheightshotel	

Bambury's Guest House

DINGLE

Apart from the amazing scenery, the Dingle peninsula has one of the greatest concentrations of tremenduously interesting Celtic ruins, Ringforts, Beehives and stone crosses. There is in fact something of interest for everyone visiting Dingle and the town itself, which used to be an old Spanish trading port, is amazing to walk around with a great sense of atmosphere and history.

BAMBURY'S GUEST HOUSE

I was looking at a picture of Paris Hilton arriving at Dublin Airport. She got into her limo and hugged her pillow. She is not alone for many famous movie and rock stars bring their pillow with them everywhere they go. After twenty years on the road visiting hotels, guesthouses and B&B's, believe me I know why. There is nothing worse than a bad night's sleep on a cheap pillow – your day – indeed your stay can be destroyed.

This will not happen you at Bernie Bambury's beautiful Guest House for you will be in the lap of luxury and comfort. The house is only one minute away from Dingle Town Centre so you can abandon the car and just walk around the town visiting all the little boutiques, chocolate shops, and art galleries … not to mention the pubs. Bernie will be able to advise you on everywhere to visit. Dingle is in the Gaeltacht, she and her family speak Irish in the home – but

they speak English too of course.

There is a warm welcoming feel to Bambury's that is reflected in the comfortable cream and pink sittingroom where guests can relax and get to meet one another after the day's touring. There are twelve bedrooms and all are outstandingly comfortable, airy, bright and fresh, with colour televisions, direct dial telephones, tea and coffee making facilities.

In the morning you can look forward to a delicious breakfast with an enormous selection of goodies. I don't know about you but I tend to have things when I am away that I wouldn't have time to do myself at home like those gorgeous freshly baked warm scones that Bernie seems to rattle up without any bother. You have to have the hot Irish oatmeal – or porridge as we Irish know it – maybe with a drizzle of honey or something stronger!! I love too the fruit filled pancakes with maple syrup … and then I always seem to have the smoked salmon with scrambled eggs.

Paris Hilton should visit Bambury's she wouldn't need her own pillow!

Owners	Bernie Bambury
Address	Mail Road, Dingle,
	Co. Kerry.
Tel	066 9151244
No of Rooms	12
Price	
Double/twin	€120
Family	€150
Dinner	No
Open	All Year
Credit Cards	Yes
Directions	On the N86 on the left after a Gas Station on the edge of Dingle Town - about one minute walk from Dingle
Email	info@bamburysguesthouse.com
Web	
www.lucindaosullivan.com/bamburysguesthouse	

The Brook Lane Hotel

Kenmare is a fantastic town to which people gravitate in search of good food and fun and they will find it in abundance. Kenmare, or to give it its Irish name "Neidin", has lots of shops, boutiques, galleries, decent places to eat, and pubs by the score, you will never be bored in Kenmare.

THE BROOK LANE HOTEL

A very welcome addition to Kenmare is the stylish new boutique Brook Lane Hotel, which adds an urban chic dimension to the accommodation sector, having superb rooms and doing excellent modern food. The Brook Lane is very conveniently located on the corner of the road leading to, or from, Sneem and the Ring of Kerry, which means that you are very close to the centre of town. All you have to do is dump your car and stroll around "doing" the boutiques, galleries and pubs, without worrying whether you will find a parking space or not – Kenmare is a busy spot.

The Hotel has been done with immense panache – cool and contemporary – and unlike anywhere else that I can think of in Kenmare. It is what today's traveller wants and deserves in the line of comfort and luxury without being overly expensive. The bedrooms are gorgeous, beds to get lost in, fluffy robes and heated bathroom floors to keep your toes warm. Whether your room is Superior, Deluxe or a Junior Suite, you can't go wrong. Colours are neutral with lots of big brown leather cosy chairs to settle into and the service is excellent and friendly. They have just recently added a new meeting room with multimedia projector and connection, remote control air conditioner, retractable overhead screen, plus, of course, wireless Internet access.

There is plenty of good casual food served all day in their cool Casey's Bar and Bistro, which is very attractively finished using lots of brick detail, and where you can very comfortably perch at the bar for that pint or a cocktail. Having perhaps just done the Ring of Kerry you will be hungry so for dinner you can start thinking of delicious pan-fried scallops on ginger bread, followed maybe by monkfish with a chilli and coriander cream, or roast breast of Aylesbury duck on hot and sour cabbage. In summer, Irish Nights (not every night so do enquire when booking) are organised for diners and you may well get to see a Bodhran, a traditional Irish musical instrument, being played. So at The Brook Lane you will get the very best of chic modern hospitality with a bit of tradition thrown in for good measure.

Owners	Dermot Brennan
Address	Kenmare, Co. Kerry.
Tel	064 42077
Rooms	20
Price	
Double/Twin	€110 - €190
Single	€110
Family	€130 - €170
Dinner	Yes – Bar food and Restaurant
Open	All Year – Closed 23rd – 27th December
Credit Cards	Visa MC Amex Diners Laser
Directions	On the corner at the junction of the N70/N71
Email:	info@brooklanehotel.com
Web:	www.brooklanehotel.com

The Butler Arms Hotel

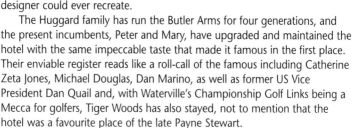

As you drive down into Waterville, on the southern point of the Ring of Kerry, there is an air of stillness, lushness and beauty. Waterville looks out to the Atlantic but there is also an unspoken eternal sultry drama and amazing colour to the backdrop of mountains. Perhaps this is what appealed to one of the most famous movie stars of all time, Charlie Chaplin, who every summer took his large family here for their annual holidays. With undoubted good taste, they stayed at the Butler Arms Hotel spectacularly located right in the middle of Waterville with views that no set designer could ever recreate.

The Huggard family has run the Butler Arms for four generations, and the present incumbents, Peter and Mary, have upgraded and maintained the hotel with the same impeccable taste that made it famous in the first place. Their enviable register reads like a roll-call of the famous including Catherine Zeta Jones, Michael Douglas, Dan Marino, as well as former US Vice President Dan Quail and, with Waterville's Championship Golf Links being a Mecca for golfers, Tiger Woods has also stayed, not to mention that the hotel was a favourite place of the late Payne Stewart.

I love everything about the Butler Arms, the beautifully restrained and impeccable bedrooms, the Charlie Chaplin lounge where I crash out and catch up on my reading, breaking for a casual lunch in the Fisherman's Bar, but saving myself somewhat for the goodies that will be available in the Fisherman's Restaurant for Dinner! The food is excellent and you can indulge yourself with lobster or wild salmon from Lough Currane or, if you are a real

carnivore, there is the best of Kerry Mountain lamb … the menu is always extensive and you won't be disappointed.

So don't just whiz around the Ring of Kerry like the coach tours, make Waterville your destination and stay and enjoy its spectacular beauty and interesting spots. The home of the Emancipator, Daniel O'Connell, just six miles away at Derrynane Bay is well worth a visit and there are dozens of ancient forts and standing stones. Ballinskelligs too is nearby or you could take a boat trip to the Skelligs.

Peter, Mary and the next generation, daughter Louise, who is now the Manager, will ensure you have a wonderful time at the Butler Arms.

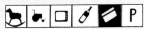

Owners:	Peter and Mary Huggard
Address:	Waterville, Co. Kerry.
Tel	066 9474144
No. Of Rooms	40
Price	
Junior Suite	€250-350
Double/Twin	€180-€250
Single	€100-€150
Dinner	Yes - Restaurant and Bar Food
Open	April to October
Credit Cards	Visa MC Amex Laser
Directions	In the centre of Waterville
Email	reservations@butlerarms.com
Web	www.lucindaosullivan.com/butlerarms

Cahernane House Hotel

My first introduction to the Cahernane House Hotel was over twenty years ago when my better half and I went there for a weekend. At that stage some German people owned it. I particularly remember our lovely room to the back of the house with ivy-clad walls, overlooking beautiful countryside and lawns. We decided to go for a stroll around the grounds but discovered that there was a pet fox in a wire compound and apparently he was on a diet of live rabbit, which ended our stroll rather rapidly! Since that time of course things have changed in a big way. It is now a spankingly beautiful Country House Hotel stunningly located and I have always had a great affection for it

The former home of the Earls of Pembroke this gorgeous old historic house is at the end of the long tree-lined drive sheltered away from the world yet close to everything, just like being on one's own private estate. The Earls of Pembroke came to Ireland in 1656. One brother was given the great Muckross Estate and the other the smaller property of Currens and Cahernane, and they maintained these magnificent Estates for five generations. In 1877 the original house was considered outmoded, torn down and replaced with the beautiful house which stands today.

Located on the Kenmare road just 1.5 kms from Killarney town centre, Cahernane House has undergone a magnificent but sympathetic refurbishment providing now the ultimate in luxury, including suites and junior suites, and superb modern rooms in a new section. Do note the beautiful latticed staircase and scrumptious drawing room, they are really beautiful. Food is excellent too in their Herbert Room Restaurant. We had delicious pan-fried medallions of veal with a wild mushroom and garlic mustard cream on our visit followed by scrumptious pear and almond tart. The wine list is extensive and they also do excellent casual food in the Cellar Bar – delicious seafood chowder, white crabmeat salad and also a lovely Country House Salad of mixed leaves, smoked bacon, poached egg, and asparagus. Being run now by the Brown family, Cahernane House Hotel has the benefit of personal and dedicated attention to make your visit the best. It is a lovely romantic spot and there is just something about Cahernane that draws you back.

The Earls of Pembroke sure knew how to pick a location!

Owners	The Browne Family
Address	Muckross Road, Killarney, Co. Kerry.
Tel	064 31895
No. Of Rooms	38
Price	
Double/Twin	€190 - €299
Family	As above + €30 B&B per child
Single	€150 - €255
Dinner	Yes - Restaurant
Open	1st February – 30th November
Credit Cards	Visa MC Amex Diners Laser
Directions	From Killarney Town follow the Kenmare Road for 1.5km. Hotel entrance is on the right.
Email:	info@cahernane.com
Web:	www.lucindaosullivan.com/cahernane

Carrig
Country House

CARAGH LAKE

Caragh Lake is a lush magnificent area virtually hidden away from the Tourist be they Irish or otherwise. It has however been a popular area for many years with the Germans a number of whom bought houses in the 1960's.

CARRIG COUNTRY HOUSE

We discovered Carrig Country House, an original 19th C. hunting lodge, at Caragh Lake in 1997 quite by accident when we arrived out there disheveled, distraught and hungry, with two young boys on tow. We were staying in a dreadful B. & B. in Killorglin, which had thimbles of watery orange juice for breakfast and brown psychedelic sheets from the 1970's and we nearly cried when we realized we could have been in luxury in Carrig House had we but known of it. We couldn't find anywhere to eat and were at one another's throats when a young girl had told us about "the new house out at the lake". Off we took like the clappers, 4 miles out of Killorglin, to find there was a God, and Heaven awaited in the shape of the welcoming Frank Slattery, and his wife Mary, who had opened for business that summer. Even if we couldn't stay there on that occasion, at least we were able to have dinner in the magnificent William Morris papered diningroom overlooking the mysterious lake with its mountainous background. We did however return again and it was as blissful as we had first thought. Arthur Rose Vincent chose Carrig House in which to live after

his former residence, Muckross Estate in Killarney, was made over to the Irish State by his American father in law, following the death of his young wife. Arthur clearly had an eye for beauty. The 4 acres of gardens have 935 different species of mature trees and plants, including some very rare and exotic varieties, and are just divine. Dingly dell, mixes with rolling lawns sweeping down to the private jetty which has boats for fishing or just for guests' pleasure. Splendid new rooms have been added at Carrig including a Presidential Suite. The food is fabulous and Frank and Mary, while professional to their fingertips, are just fun. People relax and there is laughter and buzz at Carrig. We had torn ourselves reluctantly away and, as we drove out the gates, My Beloved surprisingly broke into verse, "I come from haunts of coot and hern, I make a sudden sally..."

Owners	Frank & Mary Slattery,
Address	Caragh Lake, Killorglin, Co. Kerry.
Tel/Fax	066 9769100
No. Of Rooms	16
Price	
Suites	€230 - €375
Double/Twin	€130 - €220
	Family Extra bed in room €40 pp
Dinner	Yes
Open	Early March – Early December
Credit Cards	All Major Cards
Directions	Left after 2.5 miles on N70 Killorglin-Glenbeigh Road (Ring Of Kerry)
Email	info@carrighouse.com
Web	www.lucindaosullivan.com/carrighouse

Castlewood House

DINGLE

The Dingle peninsula is so intensely shatteringly beautiful that one can almost feel its raging tempestuous undercurrent churning away. The movie "Ryan's Daughter" brought people from all over the world to Dingle and they still come in their droves including one who has remained for some time - Fungi the dolphin, who is undoubtedly Dingle's most famous resident.

CASTLEWOOD HOUSE

Brian and Helen Heaton are a young couple who have brought their wealth of style, and experience at the upper end of the hospitality industry, into their spanking brand new Castlewood House, which has to be one of the finest Guest Houses I have ever been in.

Custom built to their very discerning specifications, Castlewood offers the guest the ultimate in luxury accommodation, the equivalent of any of the finest 5 star hotels, but of course at a fraction of 5 Star Hotel prices. Castlewood curves gently demi lune style overlooking Dingle Bay and all of the bedrooms have magnificent views of the water. Each bedroom is individually themed, an Oriental room, a French room, and so on – all equally gorgeous – for which Brian and Helen spent months buying here and abroad for all of the special little details. Each room also has a CD/DVD player, satellite TV, mini fridge, Internet access, hospitality trays, and the

lovely bathrooms have whirlpool baths and power showers.

From the moment you cross the doorstep into the wide elegant hall with curved staircase and double doors to the drawingroom and diningroom you realise it is magnificently furnished with beautiful antiques and paintings. The drawingroom is splendid, the diningroom lovely, you won't want to leave here. Helen has superb taste perhaps inherited from her mother, who is a distinguished Artist and some of her work can be seen on the walls of Castlewood.

You will enjoy breakfast overlooking the water. The buffet is lavish with a beautiful selection of fruits, cereals, cheeses, charcuterie, and scrumptious breads and pastries. The pancakes with a fruit topping and maple syrup are sinful as is Helen's creamed porridge with local organic honey or Bailey's. The delicious smoked salmon omelettes are another option – don't worry for the Full Irish is there too – Brian makes sure of that as well as a Fresh Fish of the Day option.

Brian and Helen are a charming and helpful young couple and will really add to the pleasure of your holiday.

Owners	Brian and Helen Heaton
Address	The Wood, Dingle, Co. Kerry.
Tel	066 9152788
No. Of Rooms	12
Price	
Double/Twin	€150
Single	€110
Family	€180
Dinner	No
Open	February to December
Credit Cards	Visa MC Diners Laser
Directions	Located 500m from Dingle Town. Take main road towards Milltown, last house on right.
Email	castlewoodhouse@eircom.net
Web	www.castlewooddingle.com

Gorman's Clifftop House

If you want to visit the most romantic setting, in one of the furthermost west establishment in Europe, you must stay at Gorman's Clifftop House at Glaise Bheag, near the small fishing village of Ballydavid, on the Slea Head Drive and Dingle Walking Way. The location has that absolute *aaaah* factor, for the stone fronted house faces out over Smerwick Harbour, Three Sisters Mountains, Sybil Head to the left, with the vastness of the Atlantic beyond. As if that is not enough, at the back of the house you have the spectacular vista of the Brandon Mountains.

Vincent Gorman's family settled this wild and beautiful land in the 1700's but Sile only came to Dingle 25 years ago on holiday, met Vincent and fell in love, not only with him, but also with Dingle. They are the most welcoming and warm couple you could meet and you will have a brilliant time at their home.

The house is beautifully and sympathetically furnished to blend in with nature. Natural waxed pine mixes with the colours of the hedgerows and the beautiful pottery of Louis Mulcahy. Double rooms have kingsize beds whilst superior rooms have superking. There are direct dial phones, Internet access, TVs and all the amenities one could possibly want. Gorman's offer plenty of choice with room service available from 8 a.m. until 10 p.m. which is most unusual for this type of establishment.

Vincent and Sile are solicitous hosts and you will enjoy sitting around the cosy fire, sharing information, planning the next days trip, and meeting interesting people from all over the world. The diningroom faces the water and you can expect Vincent's delicious food to perhaps include crab claws with garlic butter, or traditional potato cakes with Annascaul black pudding, followed by juicy prawns or hoppingly fresh turbot, straight from the local fishing boats, served perhaps with vanilla and orange syrup with lentils. Do leave room for the chocolate cake, it is to die for.

There is nothing more magical than sitting out in Gorman's garden with a decent glass of wine listening to roar of the waves and watching the sun go down. It is a wonderful place, rejuvenating, fun, so good for the soul, and an experience you will never forget.

Owners	Vincent & Sile Gorman
Address	Glaise Bheag, Ballydavid, Dingle Peninsula, Co. Kerry.
Tel	066 9155162
No. Of Rooms	9
Price	
Double/Twin	€130 - €190
Single	€ 85 - €135
Family	€150 - €200
Dinner	Yes – Restaurant
Open	April – October
	November – March by advance reservation only
Credit Cards	Visa MC Laser
Directions	Drive through Dingle, harbour on left to roundabout,
	Straight across – signposted "An Fheothanach" –
	8 miles keep left but do not turn left.
Email	info@gormans-clifftophouse.com
Web	www.lucindaosullivan.com/gormansclifftop

Heaton's Guesthouse

We had intended setting off for Dingle early in the morning but we fell by the wayside. We had stayed at a house up at Caragh Lake, demurely had dinner beside an American couple without exchanging a word, walked around the house and came back in to the drawingroom to sit quietly in a bay window. Suddenly the door opened and a bright smiling blonde girl came in sat down and introduced herself as Marian. She and her husband, Nigel, were on their first trip to Ireland as their son was on a school rugby trip in Limerick. As often happens with English people who have no family connections with Ireland, it was their first trip here, and frankly they wouldn't have come unless they had to, for they usually went to exotic locations. We had a drink, and another drink before Nigel sensibly suggested they retire. Next morning at breakfast we all waved at one another, had little polite chats, and nodded to the Americans. We got our bags out to the car where the American couple were trying to map out their route. Telling us they had Restaurants in the States, I confessed to being probably their archenemy – a Restaurant Critic. With that a German car swung into the car park and came over to join in. On learning my occupation the German went to his car boot and took out a little fold up table, spread a check cloth, took out two bottles of wine from his region in Germany, some titbits, special knives and told us he had been coming to Ireland for over 30 years, using the same table, knives and equipment each year! Nigel and Marian emerged and we had the League of Nations Irish, English, Americans and Germans, having a party in a Car park in Kerry, They had never experienced anything like it and told us since it was the best trip of their lives. That's what Kerry and Ireland is really all about.

HEATON'S GUESTHOUSE

Cameron and Nuala Heaton's eponymous Guesthouse is spectacularly located on the edge of the water with magnificent views of Dingle Bay. There is something special about being close to the water that is infectious and life giving. The shimmering ripples are wonderful to sit by during the summer and stunningly dramatic viewed through a window in the depths of winter. Heaton's has 16 rooms, standard, deluxe and Junior Suites, take your choice, but all are beautifully draped and furnished in cool clear, up to the minute, stylish colours. Each with T.V. Tea/Coffee makers, and superb bathrooms with power-showers, are spacious and have everything you could possibly want for your comfort. There is a large foyer and a lounge sittingroom area with big comfortable sofas where you can snuggle up, cosy up, or just relax. Breakfast is served in the diningroom which also makes the most of the magnificent views with big plate glass windows. This is daughter, Jackie's, area and you can chose from an amazing selection which includes juices, fruits, cereals, stewed fruits – rhubarb or apple- porridge with a dram of Drambuie, brown sugar and cream, followed by the traditional Irish, or Catch of the day, local Smoked Salmon and scrambled egg. Preserves and breads are home-made. Children over 8 welcome. Cameron and Nuala are delightful people, as is their daughter Jackie, and superb hospitality is their middle name.

Owners	Cameron & Nuala Heaton
Address	The Wood, Dingle, Co. Kerry.
Tel	066 9152288
No. Of Rooms	16
Price	
Junior Suite	€134 -€188
Double/Twin	€90 - €134
Single	€56 - €99
Family	€120- €175
Dinner	No
Open	February 6 – January 2
Credit Cards	Visa MC
Directions	Look for Marina – Heaton's is about 600m beyond it.
Email	heatons@iol.ie
Web	www.lucindaosullivan.com/heatons

Manor West Hotel Spa
& Leisure Club

On the outskirts of Tralee, on the Killarney Road, stands the spanking new Manor West Hotel. Custom built from the ground up, this fine addition to Tralee offers contemporary 4 star comfort and service under the eagle eye of one of the best Hoteliers in the Country, General Manager Jim Feeney, who for many years oversaw the smooth running of the Great Southern Hotel at Parknasilla.

Your arrival in the cool marble spacious lobby with its magnificent paintings and prestigious and stylish lounge area leaves you in no doubt as to the good things to come. Manor West boasts 77 rooms with all the goodies one expects of a modern day hotel and there are also 10 suites on the top floor, Master, Executive or Junior, where you can either relax, or work, in the utmost luxury.

Off the spacious lobby is the Hotel's modern restaurant, The Walnut Room. Stylishly designed and buzzing with atmosphere, right in the centre is what might be called the "inner circle" two half moon sections facing one another which would make a great set for a movie. It is a lovely room and you can expect to dine on the best of Kerry produce. If you want to eat more informally there is the option of the very casual style Mercantile Bar with its flat screen TVs and self-service food area. Manor West is ideal too for families

who will love the Leisure Club facilities. There is an 18 metre swimming pool, sauna, steam room, Jacuzzi and a state of the art gymnasium. Whilst Dad is taking the kids to the pool, this is the time you can take yourself off to the Harmony Spa which has 5 treatment rooms, Laconium, Razul and Aroma Steam Room. Treat yourself to a body wrap and then take yourself off to spend his money at the nearby shopping centre! He won't know you by the time you come back!

The Hotel's easy parking and proximity to the busy commercial town of Tralee makes it an ideal base for the businessman. While, it's central location in the beautiful Kingdom of Kerry makes it the perfect base for the tourist who wishes to explore the delights of this splendid County.

Kerry is the Kingdom.

Owners	Jim Feeney (General Manager)
Address	Killarney Road, Tralee, Co. Kerry.
Tel	066 7194500
No. Of Rooms	77
Price	
Suites	From €100
Double/Twin	From €120
Single	From € 85
Family	From €130 (2 adults 2 children)
Dinner	Yes – 2 Restaurants
Open	All Year
Credit Cards	Visa MC Amex Laser
Directions	Situated on the N22 – Main Limerick/Killarney Road into Tralee Town
Email	info@manorwesthotel.ie
Web	www.lucindaosullivan.com/manorwest

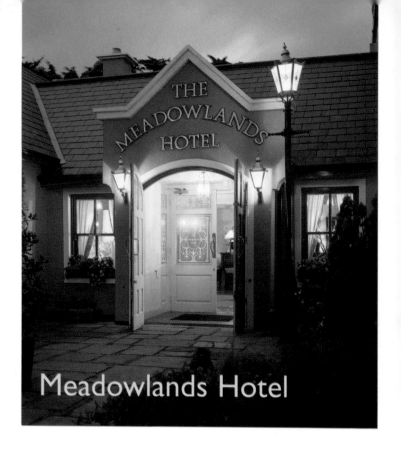

Meadowlands Hotel

"Meadowlands"? Repeated the telephone enquiry operator. "Yes", I said, "its an Hotel in Tralee". "I know", she said, "I was there last night and the food is gorgeous". Now, it wasn't the "pale moon shining" nor the fabled Rose that drew me to Tralee. Word had filtered through that the owners of Meadowlands, Padraig and Peigi O'Mathuna, were in the fish business in Dingle, "had their own trawlers", and consequently the Hotel Restaurant, "An Pota Stoir" was specializing, in beautiful fresh seafood. It was true and the whisper in the breeze was right!

The first thing that struck us about the rose coloured hotel was its spaciousness and lots of parking. The corridors are wide and the bedrooms bigger than average and very nicely decorated – beautiful heavily lined beige silk curtains, nice lamps, and furnishings and very comfortable beds. The bathrooms are very pretty, with floral painted walls, good fittings and pretty New England style doors with glass windowpanes discreetly covered with net. We came down to the Johnny Franks Bar, which is clearly very popular with local people. Modern "Traditional Irish," I suppose is how you might describe it, with a faux library at the upper level and high ceilings, lots of wood and it also does excellent barfood. The split level Pota Stoir Restaurant is casual in ethos, with lots of pine, brick, wall lights and so on, but the food and service is far from casual. There was a relaxed atmosphere as the lady pianist played away all the old favourites which lent a lovely ambience of real Ireland.

Young local man John O'Leary is the Head Chef and is clearly innovative and dedicated. You can expect to see creamy Dingle Bay seafood chowder or maybe tian of Maharees crabmeat wrapped around by a ribbon of sweet marinated cucumber and topped with shredded deep fried onion ...and the scallops with Annascaul black pudding..yum...or the panfried fillets of turbot fit ...for a prince.

Meadowlands is in a great location in Tralee, the gateway to Dingle, so you can take trips either up to Clare or further south around Kerry – a great central base.

Now you know where to bring your Rose for a bit of craic in Johnny Franks and good food in an Pota Stoir.....

Owners	Padraig and Peigi O'Mathuna
Address	Oakpark, Tralee, Co. Kerry.
Tel	066 7180444
No. Of Rooms	58
Price	
Suite	€250 - €350
Double/Twin	€170
Single	€100
Family Room	€200
Dinner	Restaurant & Bar food
Open	All Year
Credit Cards	Visa MC Amex Laser
Directions	The Hotel is situated on the N69, the Listowel Road.
Email	info@meadowlandshotel.com
Web	

www.lucindaosullivan.com/meadowlands

Muckross Park Hotel & Spa

Jackie Lavin and Bill Cullen are one of Ireland's celebrity couples. Kerry born Jackie, is long recognised as one of Ireland's beauties, as well as being an astute business woman, and Dublin born Bill Cullen wrote his incredible life story "It's a Long Way from Penny Apples", the royalties of which book, with his usual panache, Bill donated to the Irish Youth Foundation.

Some years ago Jackie and Bill bought the Muckross Park Hotel uniquely located in the National Park on the Lakes of Killarney. A hotel since 1795 and originally part of the Muckross Estate owned by the Herbert family, it has seen visitors as diverse as Michael Collins, the Liberator Daniel O'Connell and Queen Victoria. The Muckross Park Hotel was the haunt too of great writers, its informal Bistro "GB Shaw's" is named after George Bernard Shaw, who loved to stay with his wife, Charlotte Payne Townsend and, the new Atrium has hand painted wall inscriptions by W.B. Yeats and by the contemporary Irish poet, Brendan Kennelly.

There is a glorious olde world luxurious spaciousness to the entrance hall and gracious Country House reception rooms in the original house. The Piano Lounge – a perfect Victorian drawingroom - with its grand piano, magnificent sofas, beautiful fabrics, antiques and chandeliers is an oasis of calm. The Blue Pool Restaurant offers a fine dining experience whilst the bedrooms are havens of peace. I love too the little olde worlde garden just across the road.

However, the Muckross Park Hotel is not all about history for the facilities are second to none. "Molly Darcy's", their traditional Irish bar with stonewalls, wooden floors, beamed ceilings and open fires, has a great atmosphere and does excellent food virtually all day. The attentive staff were

really on the ball which is always a sign of great management. On top of this a major development plan has seen the addition of forty new superior bedrooms including four executive suites along with the addition of a sublime new Cloisters Luxury Health Spa with ten treatment rooms. Oh bliss.

So, you see, the craic is mighty, the four star deluxe facilities second to none, and now you can also pamper yourself in the magnificent Spa as part of your historical trip to Killarney.

Owners	Jackie Lavin & Bill Cullen
Address	Muckross Village,
	Lakes of Killarney,
	Co. Kerry.
Tel	064 23400
No of Rooms	69
Price	
Double/Twin	€200 - €280
Single	€130 - €170
Dinner	Yes – 2 Restaurants + Bar Food
Open	All Year
Credit Cards	Visa MC Amex Diners Laser
Directions	Take the Muckross Road to the National Park.
	Past Muckross Village on the left hand side.
	Adjacent To Muckross House & Gardens.
Email	info@muckrosspark.com
Web	www.lucindaosullivan.com/muckrosspark

    Spa NET P

Muxnaw Lodge

There is a wide variety of accommodation and high prices in Kenmare so finding that something in between can sometimes be difficult but I found just the place.

Muxnaw Lodge is a lovely gabled house, a former Hunting Lodge built in 1801 ideally situated very close to the town on the Castletownbere Road. Muxnaw is a homely but understatedly classy establishment nestled on 3 acres of fine gardens, complete with its own all weather tennis court, and enjoying outstanding views of the Kenmare River and suspension bridge. Tranquil bedrooms are all different, furnished with beautiful antiques and all have tea and coffee making facilities. Its success is a credit to the wonderful hospitality of its hostess, Hannah Boland, as well as the comforts provided. Hannah knows the area like the back of her hand and delights in mapping out routes and setting her guests off on the proper track for the day. I have indeed seen her spend many an afternoon, after she has served the most delectable afternoon tea, chatting with her guests and pouring over maps and routes, planning the remainder of their holiday.

Kenmare has any number of restaurants to tickle one's taste buds and Hannah will mark your card as to which are the best and most suitable for you. You can leave the car at Muxnaw and just stroll down the town without wondering whether you have to worry about having that second drink before you drive home. Dinner is available with advance notice and beautiful salmon cooked in the big Aga cooker is one of Hannah's specialities. There is no wine licence so you are more than welcome to bring your own. Breakfast is superb, juices, fruit, and cereals with delicious breads and followed by eggs any way you like or the Full Irish. Hannah's gentle generosity constantly shines through.

You will really feel welcome in this excellent, good value, period house in Kenmare.

Owners	Hannah Boland
Address:	Castletownbere Road, Kenmare, Co. Kerry.
Tel	064 41252
Rooms	5
Price	
Double	€90
Twin	€90
Dinner	Yes – book in advance
Open	All Year - Closed 24th and 25th December.
Credit Cards	Visa
Directions	On Castletownbere Road out of Kenmare
Email:	muxnawlodge@eircom.net
Web:	www.lucindaosullivan.com/muxnawlodge

Virginias Guesthouse

We took off, happy as sandboys, heading for Kerry with the roof rolled back on the convertible. It was a last minute trip, and as I drove along, I felt we were back in our carefree, heady, pre-nuptial days. Even His Nibs complaining that his bald patch was getting sunburned couldn't dampen our lively spirits. We sped through our favourite stretch of road, the dramatic drive between Glengarriff and Kenmare, arriving about 5 p.m. Fascinated by the interesting craft and antique shops, we strolled around for some time until, suddenly, we remembered that we had nowhere to lay our heads for the night.

It was then we discovered Virginia's Guesthouse, a rare little gem located above the popular Mulcahy's Restaurant. We were greeted like old friends by hosts Neil and Noreen Harrington. Neil was born in this house. His father was the local shoemaker and his customers had included Fred Astaire and Prince Ranier. The attraction of Virginia's is its simplicity, unpretentiousness and friendly laid back atmosphere, but with all the facilities you could require – power showers, safes, and 35 channel cable TV.

We had an excellent dinner downstairs in Mulcahy's and, what completed the perfect

day, was only having to go back upstairs to bed. The greatest test of any Guesthouse or Hotel is when you decide to stay an extra night, which we did. There was never any doubt, but the breakfast was the real clincher.

Noreen does beautiful poached seasonal fruits in a saffron cardamom and star anise syrup served with chilled organic yoghurt. Another unusual twist in her repertoire is sliced sweet pear on toasted homemade white yeast bread smothered with melted Cashel Blue cheese, served with crispy streaky bacon and homemade apple and tomato chutney. There is also, of course, the Full Irish, scrambled eggs and Kenmare smoked salmon, porridge with whiskey cream, not to mention pancakes and maple syrup. This young couple are rapidly making a name for themselves.

As they say in Kerry "We were well sorted."

Owners	Neil & Noreen Harrington
Address	36 Henry Street, Kenmare, Co. Kerry.
Tel:	064 41021
No of Rooms	8
Price	
Double/twin	€90-€120
Single	€75-85
Family	€45-60pps
Dinner	Mulcahy's Restaurant on ground floor
Open	All Year save 21st – 25th December inc
Credit Cards	Yes
Directions	2nd building on right as you drive down Henry Street, in town centre.
Email	virginias@eircom.net
Web	www.lucindaosullivan.com/virginiasguesthouse

County Kildare

Kildare county, with its lush pastureland, is a great centre for the thoroughbred horse industry. The rolling acres of the Curragh plains are a natural training ground for racehorses and the Irish Derby, one of the biggest prize races in Europe, is held on the Curragh Racecourse each year. The National Stud, famous for the breeding of outstanding racehorses is situated in Kildare Town, on the edge of the Curragh.

The county boasts numerous fine country houses and estates, remnants of the years when British gentry had their country houses in Ireland and, believe me, they knew how to select the best places. The magnificent Castletown House in Celbridge is a prime example, designed in 1722 by Alessandro Galilei. In the 1960's the Irish Georgian Society purchased the house and it was later transferred to the State in 1994, and guided tours are now available.

The Grand Canal, which runs through the county, boasts many pleasant walks along its towpaths, and Robertstown, where it divides into two branches, boasts the Grand Canal Hotel (no accommodation!!) which has a restaurant and an exhibition about the canal and the Hotel. Barge tours for groups can be arranged here.

Nearer Dublin, Maynooth is reachable by bus from the city. For many years the Roman Catholic Seminary at Maynooth was basically the headquarters of the Catholic Church in Ireland. While still a seminary, it is also part of the National University of Ireland.

At one end of Maynooth main street stands Carton House – a Georgian gem designed by Richard Cassels – which has now opened its doors as a Hotel and restaurant.

"I just played a horse yesterday so slow the jockety kept a diary of the trip"

(Henny Youngman)

144

Carton House

We have been fair deluged with openings in recent times of Country Estate Hotels with de rigueur Spa and Golf Course. Where else can the Celtic Tigresses and Yummy Mummies show off their Convertibles, 4 x 4s, Bentley's, Botoxed, toned and tanned bodies, and tarted up little terrors. Some are good, some are terrible, and some are terrific – which leads me to the magnificent Carton House at Maynooth. You can crash out in the Spa or slip off and shop 'til you drop in Grafton Street whilst he plays golf on one of the two superb courses, designed by Mark O'Meara and Colin Montgomery.

Carton and Castletown are the two Great Houses familiar to Dubliners, and oft the destination of the Sunday Drive as kids. They were inextricably linked being homes of the famous historic Fitzgerald family and the setting for the stunning BBC television series The Aristocrats. Carton House, built in 1739, is absolutely magnificent and you will be agog at the glorious reception rooms and amazing stucco work done by the Lafranchini brothers. You can almost hear the rustle of silk ballgowns and soft slippers of bewigged servants…

The sleek stylish ultra modern extension incorporates the old stonework and, in many areas, captures the wonderful serene feel of the formal gardens and great estate bringing it forward into a new era. Bedrooms are contemporary and smart with extra space allotted to the bathrooms, with both walk in shower and bath, and to the dressing area. The new foyer has a fantastic geometrically designed glass ceiling, ultra modern paintings and sofas, and to sit here at night under twinkling lights is just a delight.

In the Linden Tree Restaurant the food is seriously good and prices are very moderate for this excellence. I had a superb "Summer Salad of Fresh Lobster" followed by fab Seared Scallops circled around a tian of delicious potatoes layered with crispy pancetta. Save space for their Eton Mess. Buffet style breakfast is brilliant with an extensive selection of pastries, cheeses, charcuterie, artisan breads, fruits, the Full Irish fixings – and lashings of it. You can also dine in the nearby Club House or have casual food in the Kitchen Bar. Go to Carton – it's smart – it's hip.

Owner	James Tynan (General Manager)
Address	Maynooth, Co. Kildare.
Tel	01 5052000
No of Rooms	165
Price	
Double/twin	€170 - €310
Single	€155 - €295
Dinner	Yes – Restaurant and Barfood
Open	All Year
Credit Cards	Yes
Directions	From Dublin, take N4 westbound. Exit at "Leixlip West" and follow signs to Carton House.
Email	reservations@cartonhouse.com
Web	www.lucindaosullivan.com/cartonhouse

County Kilkenny

Kilkenny is a county of rich farmland, quaint villages and towns, well endowed with mediaeval ruins and friendly people who are not reluctant to talk about hurling, the very special Gaelic game at which Kilkenny people excel. Kilkenny City, on the River Nore, is a bustling busy place defined by the magnificent Kilkenny Castle, former home to the Butlers of Ormonde. The City has many hotels, guesthouses and bars and is very popular now for weekend breaks and for stag and hen parties. The surrounding county is not short on items of historical interest like Kilcree Round Tower, Jerpoint Abbey, and the ruin of Kells Priory. Go to Graiguenamanagh on the River Barrow, the home of Duiske Abbey, founded in 1204, and although much altered over the years the 13th Century interior has been lovingly preserved. Bennettsbridge, an area now home to many craft industries such as the Nicholas Mosse Pottery, is worth a visit, as is Thomastown, just north of Jerpoint, formerly a walled town of some importance, and close to the magnificent Championship Golf Course of Mount Juliet. Relax with a glass of Guinness, or whatever, in the tree lined square, or by the river, of interesting Inistiogue, which is overlooked by the ruin of the Woodstock Estate, burned down in 1922. Kilkenny is a fabulous county.

"I have made an important discovery...that alcohol, taken in sufficient quantities, produces all the effects of intoxication".
(OSCAR WILDE)

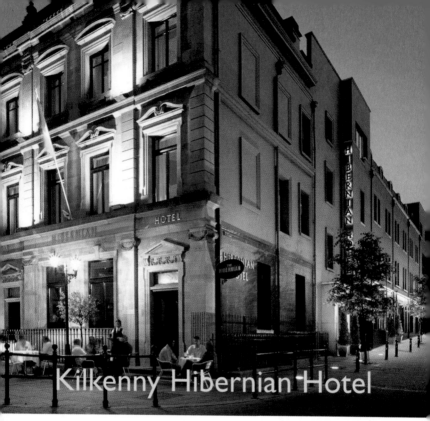

Kilkenny Hibernian Hotel

Kilkenny as a City and as a County rocks as far as I am concerned but I guess I am kind of biased as I have a Kilkenny background. Known as the Marble City, Kilkenny is filled with historic places to visit, restaurants and bars, lush hinterland, and to boot a magnificent Castle which glows goldenly over the City and its warm hearted people. I grew up on stories of the great and the good – Kilkenny Hunt, the shooting parties, the merchant princes of the City who lived in fine houses in the shadow of the Castle or on fine country estates …

One solid historic house which would have been a bastion of the "upstairs downstairs" era was No. 1 Ormonde Street, built in the mid 19th C., and lived in by the Hackett family – friends and supporters of the Liberator – Charles Stuart Parnell. In later years the building was bought by the Hibernian Bank. In 2000 it opened as a snazzy Boutique Hotel and immediately made its mark on all fronts – great rooms – great style – great restaurant – the destination of the discerning – and all under one roof. In 2007 the Hibernian has gone from strength to strength. It has been voted one of the Best Loved Hotels in the World. The bedrooms are lavishly and richly furnished and, if you really want to push out the boat, you can treat yourself to a Junior Suite or even look out over Kilkenny from the Penthouse Suite.

There are lots of restaurants in Kilkenny but Jacob's Cottage restaurant in the Hibernian is considered by many to be one of the best around. The

cuisine is modern Irish and they specialize in seafood – so you can expect maybe to feast on delicious Duncannon chowder or mussels or prawns, followed maybe by whole roast sea-bass; grilled sole on the bone and lots more. However, whilst they specialize in fish there is also plenty for the

man who likes his meat – delicious fillets of Angus beef, and plenty of game in season – I love their Marinated Haunch of Wild Venison which they serve with a root vegetable mash and a redcurrant and rosemary jus. Save space for their Warm Sticky Date Pudding … They also do bar food in their Hibernian Bar to the front of the hotel and, if you are a night owl, their fab subterranean Morrisson's Bar, which is on two floors with lots of snugs and big cozy leather sofas, will welcome you into the night with entertainment and live music.

Get thee to the Kilkenny Hibernian - don't miss out.

Owners	John McNena
	General Manager
Address	1 Ormonde Street, Kilkenny.
Te	056 7771888
No of Rooms	46
Price	
Suite	€270
Junior Suite	€230
Double/twin	From €198 (BBD packages also available)
Dinner	Restaurant and bar food
Open	All Year (Closed Christmas Eve to St. Stephen's Day)
Credit Cards	Yes
Directions	Follow signs for City Centre. Hotel is located right in the Centre.
Email	info@kilkennyhibernianhotel.com
Web	www.lucindaosullivan.com/kilkennyhibernianhotel

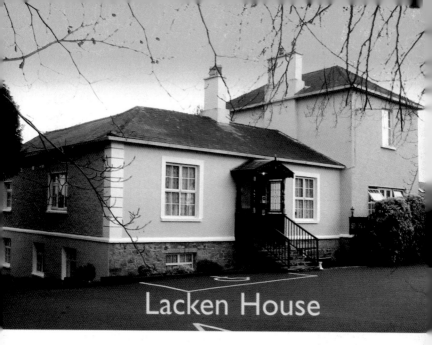

Lacken House

Well, I guess I am kind of biased when it comes to Lacken House because my father lived there as a child so it, and Kilkenny City, have a tremendous sentimental attachment for me. In fact it's a bit like a magnet, I can't stay away from the Marble City and County.

Kilkenny is Ireland's finest medieval city. There is just so much to do and see. The Castle, which dominates and creates a magical atmosphere, is a "must see" for all visitors – the silk lined walls, furnishings and paintings are glorious. The other "must see" is the 13th C. St. Canice's Cathedral. Nowadays Kilkenny is a hopping vibrant place and very popular for weekend breaks. There are lots of pubs, restaurants, hotels, galleries and shops but the trick is to find that Great Place to Stay with individual attention and good food.

Lacken House is a lovely Victorian house, built as a Dower House in 1847 for Viscount Montmorency. It is run magnificently by a young husband and wife team, Trevor Toner and Jackie Kennedy Toner, who have transformed it into a superb boutique Guesthouse. Food is a feature at Lacken House so book dinner when making your reservation – this is seriously good luxurious food . Having secured your place at the table, you can then turn your thoughts perhaps to pan seared foie gras wrapped in duck magret served with caramelised banana and truffled honey or, you might fancy starting with panfried hake on squid ink risotto with sautéed scallop and clams. When you have whetted your appetite on either of those you can concentrate on the main courses which might include tender fillet of beef with spinach and celeriac, poached oyster, wholegrain mustard and Guinness reduction but there will be a wide choice and an excellent wine list. After that lot you can retire to the drawingroom for a nightcap by the blazing fire

before cosying up in the delightful bedrooms, which have been totally revamped by Trevor and Jackie, all now having big beds, beautiful Italian fabric wallpapers, luxurious carpets and everything else one might want.

Also available in-room (book in advance) are Holistic Massage Treatments by a registered practitioner – so pamper yourself if he disappears to play golf. By the way if you want a private tour of Kilkenny or an airport pick up in an airconditioned Mercedes 8 seater Trever and Jackie will organise that too from Lacken House.

Lacken House is the perfect place for that perfect break in perfectly beautiful Kilkenny

Owners	Trevor and Jackie Kennedy Toner
Address	Dublin Road, Kilkenny City, Co. Kilkenny.
Tel	056 7761085
No. Of Rooms	10
Price	
Double/Twin	€190
Single	€95
Family	€225 (up to 3 children)
Dinner	Restaurant
Open	All Year – Closed 24th – 27th December
Credit Cards	Visa MC Amex Laser
Directions	Located on N10 in Kilkenny City on main Dublin/Carlow Road.
Emai	info@lackenhouse.ie
Web	www.lucindaosullivan.com/lackenhouse

Langton House Hotel

Kilkenny City is a hot hot destination for young and old alike. It has a zing and zest in mediaeval surroundings that are second to none. I had visiting journalists over from the U.S. during the summer and they were gobsmacked when they visited the new Langton House Hotel in Kilkenny. Their eyes were out on stalks when they saw the restaurant and the bars – "more stunning than anything in New York", they gushed.

The Langton name has always been synonymous with good food in Kilkenny. Ask anyone and they will tell you the same. In fact the "Edward Langton's Bar" won the Black & White overall Pub of the Year Award a record four times. I am mentioning this merely to tell you that Langton's have always been conscious of providing excellent service and quality but, if I said the Langton Group had moved up a notch or two, that would be putting it mildly, for they have moved up into a new stratosphere with their fabulous Langton House Hotel, their visually stunning Langton Room restaurant, and their uber cool new Carrigan's Bar, which has been designed by fashionable London based Irish designer David Collins.

Situated right at the heart of the City near the Castle, Langton's has 30 fab new oversized rooms and suites to accommodate all needs be it the Penthouse Suites, Executive Suites, Club Family Suites, Superior Garden Suites, Double/Twin Rooms … each and every one stylishly equipped for today's

discerning clientele. There is cable television, mini-bars, private safes, surround sound stereo entertainment systems, 24 hour room service and wireless internet access (request at check-in).

Believe me you are never going to be bored at Langton's for in the hotel they have the 67 Bar where throughout the week they have live entertainment through traditional music to bands and dj's. There is also Harry's Bar, the Middle Bar and the beautiful Ballroom Bar. You will never be hungry for there is food everywhere but the restaurant, now that is a stunning room and good value. Think of food like succulent melt in the mouth braised shank of lamb served on a mash with its own juices, or maybe Dublin Bay Prawns in garlic butter, which comes with a Caesar salad or even panfried Barbary duck with Grand Marnier … Yum. You can't do your tour of Kilkenny, never mind your tour of Langton's emporia, without visiting The Marble City Bar – its ab fab.

Owner	Eamon Langton
Address	69 John Street, Kilkenny.
Tel	056 7765133
No of Rooms	30
Price	
Suites	€65 - €110pps
Double/twin	€65 - €110pps
Family	€65- €110pps
Dinner	Yes – Restaurant and Barfood
Open Day	All Year save Christmas
Credit Cards	Yes
Directions	On N9 from Carlow at Dublin Road roundabout take 2nd exit onto Dublin Road, Turn left onto John Street. Turn left at 2nd pedestrian crossing into private carpark.
Email	reservations@langtons.ie
Web	www.lucindaosullivan.com/langtonshousehotel

 NET P

Mount Juliet
Conrad

Mount Juliet is a magnificent Georgian Mansion built by the Earl of Carrick, overlooking the River Nore, on 1500 acres of unspoiled woodland and meandering waters in Thomastown, South Kilkenny. Latterly, Mount Juliet was owned by the late Major Victor McCalmont and his wife Bunty, well known figures on the Irish social scene. Hunting, shootin', fishin', House Parties, were the thing along, with the Dublin Horse Show, Hacking Jackets from Callaghan's of Dame Street, antiques from Louis Wine. The lives of staff in those days revolved around the big Estate and very often went from generation to generation of minding "the Major" and previous incumbents. Mount Juliet was developed with great foresight and subtlety by businessman, Tim Mahony, for even though you drive through the Jack Nicklaus designed 18 hole Championship Golf Course, past the self catering Rose Garden Lodges and Hunters Yard complex, the house is far enough away to retain the illusion of being on a private estate and still feels more "Country House" than Hotel. Now part of the Conrad Hotel Group, if your days aren't filled with golf or country pursuits, you can chill out and be pampered at the Health Club and Spa. There are two Restaurants, the Lady Helen Diningroom, with really superb food. Albert Roux the famous French Chef comes to Mount Juliet to shoot and he cooked the favourite soufflé of the late Queen Mother for us. The other dining option is Kendals Restaurant in the Hunters Yard which is large and buzzy. The rooms in the main house are gracious and beautiful and the modern rooms in the Hunters yard are super. Breakfast in the Lady Helen Room overlooking the River, rolling acres and romping young cattle, is simply bliss with a tremendous circular array of fresh, dried and exotic fruits, pastries, French yoghurts, cheeses, cold cuts, smoothies, porridge with fresh cream or honey, pancakes with maple syrup, cinnamon sugar and Wexford strawberries. "Would you like to try Tiger's Breakfast?" Asked the Restaurant Manager. I was still romancing about the classy Colonial days, *Indiaaah* and all that, forgetting that more recent blow in, Tiger Woods, until I was enlightened. Anyway, Tiger's breakfast is stacked French toast and smoked salmon topped with poached eggs. You might fancy "The Major's breakfast" which delves into the nether regions of liver and kidneys – strong stuff first thing. Mount Juliet is a glorious place, it is not just the house and nice staff, but the lushness of the grounds and winding paths which are a constant reminder of another life – people crave peace and space they will find it all here. Best rates available online at www.conradhotels.com. It is the finest Country Estate in Ireland.

Owners	William Kirby (General Manager)
Address	Thomastown, Co. Kilkenny.
Tel	056 7773000
No. Of Rooms	58
Price	
Double/Twin	From €189
Single	From €172
Family	From €380 – Rose Garden Lodge
Dinner	Yes – 2 Restaurants
Open	All Year
Credit Cards	All Major Cards
Directions	Follow signs from Thomastown
Email	info@mountjuliet.ie
Web	

www.lucindaosullivan.com/mountjuliet

Spa | 18h | NET | H | P

County Limerick

Limerick City, located at the lowest fording point of the River Shannon, is sports mad whether it be Gaelic football, hurling, horse racing, soccer or particularly rugby football which boasts that well known Limerick invention the "Garryowen":- the high kick forward which allows your team to charge after it and put the fear of God into the poor player who happens to be trying to catch it. It is also famous as the location of Frank McCourt's book *Angela's Ashes*, although some of its inhabitants find it hard to accept. From the time the Vikings sailed up the Shannon and settled there, the place has had a troubled

history but it is probably best remembered for the Williamite Siege in the late 1600's resisted by the Irish, led by Patrick Sarsfield. Probably the best-known tourist attraction in the city is the Hunt Museum, which has a collection to rival Dublin's National Gallery. In the late 1930's and early 1940's, Foynes was the terminus for the transatlantic Flying Boat service, and is home now to a Flying Boat Museum. Kilmallock and its nearby Museum is only four miles from Bruree, whose claim to fame is that it was the childhood home of Eamonn de Valera, former prominent 1916 figure, Taoiseach, and President of Ireland. The gem in the county's crown is the beautiful picturesque village of Adare which has many up market fine antique shops, friendly pubs, excellent Restaurants and art shops but also has a number of beautifully maintained thatched cottages and is regarded as the prettiest village in Ireland.

"The one duty we have to history is to re-write it"
(OSCAR WILDE)

Dunraven Arms Hotel

Every November I look forward to an Invitation from my Horsey friends to The Hunt Ball in Adare. Whilst a night of Tallyho with The Equine Fraternity of Limerick has its own special appeal, the real appeal for His Nibs and myself is to escape to Irelands prettiest village and stay in The Dunraven Arms, which never disappoints. This year was no exception and, even though it was a bleak mid winter day when we descended on Adare, the village looked stunning with its many thatched cottages, up market restaurants, funky art galleries, and serious Antique Shops. The Dunraven Arms with its richly painted walls and limestone trims stands out like a beacon of light and welcome in Adare. Built in 1792, The Dunraven Arms is wonderfully stylish and one is always assured of a warm welcome, as well as all the advantages of modern creature comforts and modern technology. There is complimentary WIFI access throughout the hotel which is brilliant nowadays. We arrived in the early afternoon in time for a swim in the leisure centre and for me a facial. Our rooms were beautifully furnished and filled with every creature comfort, Bliss. Suites and Junior Suites are superb with

ample seating areas and dressing rooms. I have had many an encounter with shoddy service delivered by souls that possess what I call "The After the Party Look", not so in Dunraven Arms. There was an abundance of extremely well groomed, well trained and very helpful staff to cater to our every whim. On the morning after, when we trundled down to breakfast, many of us bearing the aforementioned "After The Party Look" there was a feast of freshly squeezed juices of all types, platters of fruit, bowls of cereals, steaming hot silver pots of tea, and lovely breads but, best of all, hidden under a silver dome was the most delicious baked ham which is their Sunday morning speciality. From all my friends who have stayed in the Dunraven Arms I have never heard anything but high praise and, I can guarantee you that I would walk barefoot on broken glass back to The Dunraven Arms just for a sliver of that honey baked ham. The food is wonderful, the service is excellent, and the location is stunning. Golly gosh old boy, an all round corker!

Owners	Louis Murphy
Address	Adare, Co. Limerick.
Tel	061 396633
No. Of Rooms	86 Bedrooms inc 30 Suites
Price	Suite/Junior Suite From €250
Double/Twin	From €185
Single	From €165
Dinner	Yes – 2 Restaurants
Open	All Year
Credit Cards	All Major Cards
Directions	On right as you enter Adare Village from N21 from Limerick direction.
Email:	reservations@dunravenhotel.com
Web:	www.lucindaosullivan.com/dunravenarms

County Mayo

ayo is a beautiful county with a landscape of high cliffs, lonely mountains and fuchsia hedges and is renowned as the home of Grace O'Malley, the notorious female pirate, rustler, and rebel whose story is a book in itself. Grace's stronghold was at Clew Bay, which is close to the Pilgrim Mountain of Croagh Patrick, the highest mountain in the area. It is from this spot that Ireland's patron Saint is said to have rid the country of snakes. Off to the east, situated snugly between Lough Conn and Lough Cullin is Pontoon, an ideal base for exploring the shores of the lakes or for casting a fishing line. Further east is Knock, well known for its shrine and apparition but now also known for the International Airport at Charlestown nearby. In the south is Cong, site of the ruined 12th Century

Cong Abbey, and where the mountains of Connemara give way to the fertile farmland of east Mayo. Probably the best-known centre in Mayo is the Georgian town of Westport, a popular playground for travelers who wish to get away from the wild western countryside. During the summer the town is very popular with visitors from all over Europe and the United States who return annually to enjoy once again its many charms and also to take in its Art Festival.

Ardmore Country House Hotel

Having travelled the length and breath of Ireland, I know only too well that wherever you stay can literally make or break your visit and leave an indelible memory. Unfortunately, my first visit to Westport was destroyed by rude receptionists, a stained bed, a dirty room, and bad food and I won't even go into the after effects of that visit but it took six months to recover. Now, if we had only known of the wonderful Ardmore Country House Hotel we could have spared ourselves that disaster.

ARDMORE COUNTRY HOUSE HOTEL

Westport is a busy tourist orientated Town, very pretty, lying on the water, within the shadows of a Great House - the famous 18th C. Westport House belonging to the Altamont family. Just 3 kms from the centre of the town is Pat and Noreen Hoban's Ardmore Country House. Stunningly located overlooking Clew Bay, Ardmore House is in the shadow of Croagh Patrick, enjoying breathtaking sunsets, and is within walking distance of the gates of Westport House. The 13 very large and spacious bedrooms are dramatically and stylishly furnished with luxurious fabrics, wonderful colours, and have all the little extras, one expects nowadays in top hotels, including a turndown service, power shower and good toiletries. Bedroom prices vary depending on whether they are to the front of the house with those spectacular sea views, or have a rural outlook to the rear. Open fires and a tinkling grand piano are what you can expect to enjoy at Ardmore after you have enjoyed a lovely meal in the Restaurant – it's a grown up place and not

suitable for children under 12. Pat Hoban is a fine chef so you can expect to enjoy spanking fresh seafood from Clew Bay, including scallops, and lobster when available. Carnivores are not ignored because prime Irish beef, lamb and wild foul feature too. Organic vegetables and herbs come from local producers along with an extensive selection of Irish farmhouse cheeses. There is an extensive wine list with affordable, as well as fine, wines from all the de rigueur Chateaux for the discerning connoisseur. Pat and Noreen are warm and friendly hosts who will only want to ensure that you enjoy your stay with them and see to your every comfort. Following Ardmore's inclusion in the first edition of my Little Black Book of Great Places to Stay, one visitor wrote in the Ardmore guest book "Lucinda O'Sullivan has it just right". Go and find out for yourself.

Owners	Pat Hoban
Address	The Quay, Westport, Co. Mayo.
Tel	098 25994
No. Of Rooms	13
Price	
Double/Twin	€150 - €200
Single	€100 - €150
Dinner	Yes - Restaurant
Open	March - December
Credit Cards	Visa MC Amex
Directions	Leave Westport on R335 Louisburg/Coast road for 3 km, watch for sign.
Email	ardmorehotel@eircom.net
Web	www.lucindaosullivan.com/ardmorehousehotel

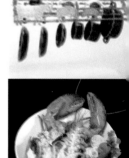

Ashford Castle

The former country home of the Guinness family, Ashford Castle is on 350 acres of the most beautiful grounds, walks and lakes, and is incredibly romantic and evocative. It was founded in the 13th C and through the centuries had had various additions, the most signaficant being a French Chateau section in 1715. The guest book reads like a roll call of the world's most famous people – Princess Grace, Tony Blair, John Ford, John Wayne, Bob Hope, Ronald Reagan, Fred Astaire, and George V of England. Pierce Brosnan and his wife Keely chose it for their wedding. However, you do not have to have your name in lights or be mega rich to enjoy Ashford Castle for they also do wonderful special breaks at certain times of the year. There is so much to do within the estate – a 9 hole golf course, fishing, clay pigeon shooting, horseriding, health spa and beauty centre and the school of falconry is an incredible experience, not to be missed. Walks through the woods with these birds will bring you straight back to Lancelot and Guinevere. This too is "Quiet Man" country and "Squire Danagher's" house is on the estate.

The magnificent oak panelled halls lead to a central drawingroom, the social hub of the castle. On our first evening there, we dined in the Connaught Room, considered the finest room, with its fairytale inglenook fireplace and glorious ceiling holding the most exquisite chandelier. If you want a special treat, an experience you will remember, this is it. The sublime degustation menu is prepared by Michelin starred chef, Stefan Matz, and you will be waited on with grace and style as you sit romantically facing out to the lake.

There are three other dining options at Ashford, the King George V room which is also fabulous with the most luxurious food – poached foie gras with melted figs and sauterne jellies, scallops and black pudding on creamed potatoes, and seared monkfish with Connemara lobster claw are but a few. They also have an extensive menu for kids. More casual food is served in the Drawing Room and in their latest addition "Cullens at the Cottage" which does delicious bistro food very reasonably priced. The staff are fantastic and do everything possible to make your stay perfect.

Ashford is a special experience.

Owners	Niall Rochford (General Manager)
Address	Cong, Co. Mayo.
Tel	094 9546003
No of Rooms	83
Price	
Double/twin	From €287
Single	On Request
Family	From €401
Dinner	3 Restaurants plus drawingroom menu
Open	All Year
Credit Cards	Yes

 NET 9H Spa H P

Directions	From Galway take Castlebar/Headford Road N84. Continue on through Headford and on to the village of Cross. In Cross turn left at the Church for Cong. As you drive into Cong the Castle is on your left.
Email	reservations@ashford.ie
Web	www.lucindaosullivan.com/ashfordcastle

Ballywarren Country House

David and Diane Skelton's Ballywarren Country House is straight out of Country Life. From the gracious black and white tiled hall, with its blazing fire and oak galleried staircase, the feel is of warmth and welcome. The bedrooms are scrumptious with some having handcarved or four-poster beds. Not only are they lavishly furnished but David and Diane, being the perfect hosts, make sure that you are pampered with all the goodies that might have been enjoyed by guests at old style Country house parties – short of providing you with a valet! Each bedroom has chocolates, a decanter of sherry – glossy magazines – and playing cards – though I don't think you will have much time to be sitting playing patience! The bathrooms are beautiful and equipped with Crabtree & Evelyn toiletries

After you have freshened up – and had a little secret nip of sherry – come down to the drawingroom and have a pre-dinner drink - Diane will be cooking something really delicious, of that you can be sure. It might be Donegal crab with a sweet chili sauce or Bacon and walnut salad with a walnut dressing – the walnuts being fresh from the Perigord – followed by confit of French Barbary duck leg with Sarladaise potatoes and peas with a Perigord sauce. She also does a very good braised lamb shank with red wine vegetables and herbes de Provence and a delicious canon of lamb on champ

with redcurrant gravy, or it might be seatrout or roast guinea fowl…wow. And, the breakfasts…as well as the extensive buffet table they do their own home made crepinettes – pork sausages..and oatmeal pancakes..

The house is perfection, the food is perfection, and to cap it all the location too is perfection – lakes all around – "Quiet Man" country. It is a fisherman's paradise beside Lough Corrib and Lough Mask. The rivers are jumping with fish and you won't be talking about the "one that got away". Close by is Cong village and Ashford Castle, Galway City is a mere 30 minutes away, Connemara is your oyster.

You are allowed to bring your pet but I don't mean Sammy the snake or Charlie the cheetah so discuss with David beforehand!! Children over 14 are welcome.

Ballywarren is one of Ireland's real hidden gems.

Owners	David & Diane Skelton
Address	Cross, Cong, Co. Mayo.
Tel	094 9546989
No of Rooms	3
Price	
Double	€136-€148 (Price reduction on Rose/Lavender rooms for 2 + nights.
Dinner	Yes
Open	January - December
Credit Cards	Yes
Directions	From Galway take N84 to Headford then R334 to Cross. At Cross Church fork left, Ballywarren 3/4 mile on right
Email	ballywarrenhouse@gmail.com
Web	www.lucindaosullivan.com/ballywarrenhouse

JJ Gannons

BALLINROBE

Ballinrobe is a thriving town in what is known as the Lake District of County Mayo so as you can gather that means it has an abundance of fishing lakes and rivers.

JJ GANNON'S

J J Gannon's has to be one of the best kept secrets in Ireland – until now that is! Incredibly, however JJ Gannon's has been thriving at the heart of the little old town of Ballinrobe since 1837 and is now being run by third generation John Joseph Gannon and his lovely wife Niki and oh boy have they added their stamp to the place.

Jay and Niki are determined to put JJ Gannon's on the map and they are succeeding for they are getting bouquets and praise from all quarters. They have developed and extended very rapidly into a sleek, modern, eco friendly, operation providing excellent food, accommodation and hospitality for today's discerning guests.

The bedrooms are superb. They have family rooms, junior suites and deluxe rooms equipped with superking beds, the finest cotton sheets, fluffy towels, velour bathrobes, internet access, satellite TV, and private balconies where you can sit and sip champagne while soaking in the beautiful lakes and mountains of Connemara and Tourmakeady.

On the ground floor is a super contemporary cafe bar with wooden floors, stonewalls, leather bucket style chairs and cool cubes. In the bar is

where you will first encounter Jay and Niki for they are always on hand to take care of their guests and customers. You won't actually ever go hungry at Gannon's because, apart from their lovely Red Restaurant, food is also served in the bar during the day and evening and they offer really great value for smashing food.

The menu changes daily in the Red Restaurant depending on sourcing local produce and their organic poultry and meat. Their suppliers are named on the menu, fresh fish is delivered daily, breads, jams and desserts are all made in their kitchen. The food is innovative and you can look forward to trying maybe Bluebell Falls goat's cheese terrine with marinated vegetables, red onion jam and cumin toast, followed by perhaps "Phil Gibbons" roast rack of lamb, which comes with celeriac and gratin Dauphinoise or "Martin Jennings" local beef fillet with a wild mushroom ragout, spring onion champ and red wine glace. Chef Xin Sun also does a lovely panache of seafood in a chive cream sauce. They have a well thought out wine list and a great selection of wines and champagne by the glass.

Enjoy!

Owners	Jay and Niki Gannon
Address	Main Street, Ballinrobe, Co. Mayo.
Tel	094 954 1008
No of Rooms	10
Price	
Double/twin	€120
Single	€70
Family	€150
Dinner	Yes – Restaurant and barfood
Open	All Year save Good Friday
Credit Cards	Yes
Directions	On N84. 40 mins from Galway, 25 mins from Westport or Castlebar. Knock 40 mins.
Email	info@jjgannons.com
Web	www.lucindaosullivan.com/jjgannons

Knockranny House Hotel & Spa

"I can resist anything but temptation" quotes Knockranny House Hotel of Oscar Wilde. He also said "only dull people are brilliant at breakfast." At Knockranny House Hotel in Westport you are going to yield to every temptation put before you and you are going to be dull as hell at breakfast having had a brilliant night before in their gorgeous La Fougere Restaurant and Brehon Bar.

Built in 1997 to classic Victorian style, the interior is lavishly furnished, with numerous antiques and cosy log fires to create a very warm welcoming atmosphere. The bedrooms and suites are beautiful, serene and calming with lovely soft furnishings. A classy ambience. It is the sort of place that one could settle in to very comfortably and drift into a state of total relaxation. I went down with my son Ian, who likes to climb Croagh Patrick each year - in the traditional fashion – which means in bare feet!

He didn't get this stamina from his ever loving Mama because I much prefer to be soaking my bare feet in Knockranny's Spa Salveo, which suitably enough in Latin means "to heal". I had an Exotic Lime and Ginger Salt Glow which sure sorted me out leaving my skin silky and smooth whilst Ian went off to play nine holes of golf at Mulranny, only thirty minutes away.

On both nights I am afraid we hit the Brehon Bar and, after a cracking Cosmo for me and a Coke for him, we had the most scrumptious dinner in the hotels La Fougere restaurant. It is a spectacular room with columns and is a little bit remeniscent of a 1920's ballroom in Paris. I had the most delicious warm smoked haddock, asparagus and dill tart with mixed leaves

and a balsamic reduction, followed by superb roast loin of venison on a ragout of wild mushrooms and purple potato, whilst Ian had Jerusalem artichoke and Parmesan

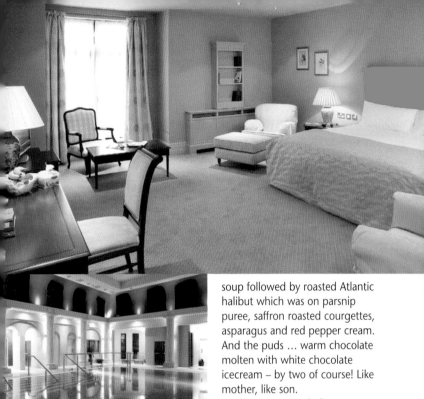

soup followed by roasted Atlantic halibut which was on parsnip puree, saffron roasted courgettes, asparagus and red pepper cream. And the puds ... warm chocolate molten with white chocolate icecream – by two of course! Like mother, like son.

Next morning before departure we hit the Connoisseur's Corner shop in the hotel and departed for Dublin with delicious breads and locally smoked salmon.

I don't think we let dear Oscar down.

Owners	Adrian and Geraldine Noonan
Address	Westport, Co. Mayo.
Tel	098 28600
No of Rooms	97
Price	
Double/twin	€210
Single	€140
Family	Yes – Sharing Under 3's free . U12's €35BB. 12-16's 35% red on adult rate.
Dinner	Yes - Restaurant
Open	All year apart from two days over Christmas
Credit Cards	Yes
Directions	Situated just off main N5 main Dublin/Castlebar/Westport road entering Westport town.
Email	info@khh.ie
Web	www.lucindaosullivan.com/knockrannyhousehotel

Pontoon Bridge Hotel

We females all love a short break away from the family with the girls and I am sure the boys too like to head off to for a bit of escapism. There is no doubt but that you return to the fray refreshed and revitalized after a few days.

Pontoon Bridge Hotel is a Mecca for anglers and people who love the water or just want a good time. It has featured on the BBC Holiday programme and on ITV's "Wish You Were Here". The location is absolutely stunning, set on a narrow peninsula right between Lough Conn and Lough Cullin, and with a gallery of mountain ranges, Nephin and Ox as a backdrop. It was bought in 1964 by Brendan and Ann Geary whose children grew up in the family business. Daughter Breeta Geary is now the General Manager, whilst her sister, Mary, apart from being Executive Chef also runs the Cookery School. Other family members are also involved ensuring a personal interest at all times. Apart from the fishing and other outdoor activities, the Pontoon Bridge Hotel run various courses from the

aforementioned cookery to landscape painting and fly fishing, all of which make great occasions for that short break. There is also excellent golf available locally. Their wonderful refurbishment programme includes Hot Tub, Sauna and Treatment rooms so that you can be thoroughly pampered.

Whatever you do, you can be sure there will be plenty to talk about over a drink in the evening after dining in any of the hotel's three restaurants – the Twin Lakes for fine dining, the Terrace Bistro and the Waterfront for Bar Food and family ambience, all with splendid views of the lake. Why not check out their mid-week and weekend packages and arrange that break now.

Owners	The Geary Family
	Breeta Geary
	(General Manager)
Address	Pontoon, Foxford,
	Co. Mayo.
Tel	094 9256120
No. Of Rooms	39
Price	
Double/Twin	€160
Single	€100
Family	€185
Dinner	Yes – 3 Restaurants
Open	All Year save 23rd –
	26th December
Credit Cards	Visa MC Amex
Directions	4 miles west of Foxford.
Email	relax@pontoonbridge.com
Web:	
www.lucindaosullivan.com/pontoonbridge	

County Meath

Meath, with its sweeping fertile pastures, is one of the richest farming areas in the country. However, it is not for the farming that the county is of such interest to the tourist, but to its wealth of interesting historical areas and remains. The famous Hill of Tara in County Meath was the seat of High Kings of Ireland for many years. Trim can boast the Ango-Norman Trim Castle, which featured prominently in the Mel Gibson movie, Braveheart. Meath is bisected by the River Boyne which gave its name to the famous battle between William of Orange with his Protestant supporters and the deposed English King, James 11, and his Catholic armies. Duchas, the Irish Heritage service, run a 30 minute tour of the battle area.

Slane Castle, although built from 1785 onwards, is probably more famous now for its massive open air Rock Concerts featuring some of the world's top stars. The nearby Hill of Slane is where the patron saint of Ireland, Patrick, lit his paschal fire at Easter 433 AD to proclaim the arrival of Christianity in Ireland. Navan, which is the main town of the county, and a busy commercial centre, is situated where the River Blackwater meets the

Boyne which was very important in the days when waterways were the chief means of transport. If you follow the River Blackwater, upstream from Navan, you come to Kells. While it is a place of monastic antiquities, it is most famous for the beautifully illuminated Book of Kells which is now on show in Trinity College in Dublin.

Probably the most interesting site in the county is Newgrange, possibly the most important Stone Age site in Europe. Built around 3000 BC, it is older than the Egyptian Pyramids and has fascinated historians and astronomers for years as to its original purpose, but was most probably an ancient burial ground with astronomical connections.

Meath, one must also record, is one of the leading Gaelic football counties in the country. This reminds me of the story of the football coach trying to exhort his players to greater efforts with roars from the sidelines "Come on Murphy, wake up, its time you got ferocious". "What number is he wearing", came Murphy's reply!

"History is too serious to be left to historians"
(Ian MacLeod, House of Commons)

Dunboyne Castle Hotel & Spa

DUNBOYNE

Dunboyne is a very pretty village in Co. Meath where we used to go many a year ago beagling with the Goldbourne Beagles. Beagling is a form of hunting on foot – in fact that is where I caught my better half! Dunboyne is now part of the commuter belt but it still retains its rural and village charm. It is a super place for a weekend break and it is also convenient for Newgrange Megalithic Passage Tomb.

DUNBOYNE CASTLE HOTEL & SPA

Dunboyne Castle Hotel & Seoid Spa made a stunning entrance onto the upmarket hotel arena in Ireland in 2006. Home to the historic aristocratic Butler family, the present castle was built in 1700's and completed in 1764 with wonderful stucco plasterwork by the famous Lafrancini Brothers. With 21 acres of grounds and formal gardens in which to relax, the whole ambience is of contemporary elegance and style. The Seoid Spa, which spans three floors, is amazing – so book yourself in for a fab weekend. The Terrace lounge overlooking the gardens is where you can enjoy afternoon tea or an aperitif before dinner, or indeed in the main Sadlier Bar. There is even a Cellar Bar where you can enjoy the craic and the singalong after dinner – or you can give them all a whirl!!

Bedrooms are state of the art scrumptious luxury – mostly set back slightly in the new wing – which in no way overshadows the beauty of the original house. This was planning and design carefully and ecologically carried out – would that it be the same everywhere. Stand outside the main entrance of the hotel and, if you close yours eyes slightly and cast your

imagination, you can visualize 18thC aristocracy strolling around the parklands.

Now to the superb food in the Ivy Brasserie. Think along the lines of a Torchon of Marinated Foie Gras with red onion marmalade, or maybe Swedish style Gravalax of Marinated Salmon with new potato and mustard salad. You might follow up with Seared Pave of Turbot with a light bouillabaisse with cockles and mussels, or being out with the County Set you might fancy oven Roast Squab Pigeon with roasted shallots. All delicious. Puddings are scrumptious …warm chocolate fondant …. It goes on

Dunboyne Castle is very special – you will love it.

Owners	Declan Curtis (General Manager)
Address	Dunboyne, Co. Meath.
Tel	01 8013500
No of Rooms	145
Price	
Double/twin	From €155
Single	From €130
Dinner	Yes – The Ivy Brasserie
Open	All year
Credit Cards	Yes
Directions	Take N3 exit off M50. Continue and take exit for Clonee/Dunboyne. Go through Clonee and this will bring you to Dunboyne. Drive through village and take a left at lights for Maynooth. Hotel is on your left hand side.
Email	info@dunboynecastlehotel.com
Web	

www.lucindaosullivan.com/dunboynecastle.com

Tankardstown House

had heard a report of Tankardstown House and consumed with curiosity I decided to check out whether or not its charms were exaggerated. On arriving, we skipped up the gleaming limestone steps to the open doors of this restored mansion and estate and were warmly greeted by Patricia and Bryan Conroy who are natural hosts.

This forward thinking couple have spared no expense in the impeccable restoration work of the main house and seven stylish cottages with patios which are located in the U shaped courtyard. These are no ordinary cottages but sanctuaries of comfort, furnished with the finest antiques, state of the art appliance and bathroom fittings, ever forgiving mirrors, grandmother clocks, even the most trivial details are attended to. These houses offer luxury and style and I could just visualise Pearce Brosnan settling in next door while making a movie in his home territory.

That night we wined and dined and partied in the great house to the sounds of a string quartet. As the fires roared in the main hall, drawingroom and diningroom, we languished on the decadent sofas, admired the sumptuous furnishings and rich rugs on the highly polished floors and we felt maybe we had passed through the pearly gates without realising it.

More of the finest champagne, great wines from an interesting list, and course after course of sumptuous food cooked and served by Patricia and her four charming daughters, Georgina, Roisin, Laureen, and Amber. Bryan

regaled us with stories of his recent trip climbing Mount Kilimanjaro. Later we all retired to our respective cottages and slept like babies on specially imported V1 mattresses. A fresh breakfast hamper was delivered to our door in the morning by Georgina. The guests dispersed for their various destinations – Tattersall's Sales, Newgrange, Hill of Tara, Dundalk and Drogheda – whilst we enjoyed a spell in the gym with a massage thrown in.

Later I curled up in front of the fire in my fairyland cottage and helped myself to the generous mini-bar and, on answering the gentle tap on the door, there stood Georgina again with a basket bearing a sumptuous Tankdardstown supper. This is a one of a kind special events venue. It offers total privacy, discretion, and gracious estate living to the discerning guest – all tailored to suit you.

Tankardstown is different – a world of stylish luxury

Owners	Bryan and Patricia Conroy
Address	Tankardstown House, Rathkenny Road, Slane, Co. Meath.
Tel:	041 9824621
No of Rooms	7 Cottages
Price	
1 bed Cottage	€1190 - €1680 per week (enq re nightly rates)
2 bed Cottage	€2380 - €3360 per week
Dinner	Yes – in Main House (24 hours notice required.
Open	All Year
Directions	Take Slane exit off M1 Motorway. Take N51 to Slane. Take Navan Road out of Slane; at Castle gates turn right to Kells. Go past Slane Farm Hostel (on right). At fork, keep left, Tankartdstown 2 miles on, on right.
Email	trish@tankardstown.ie
Web	www.lucindaosullivan.com/tankardstown

County Offaly

County Offaly, a midland county is bounded by the Shannon River to the northwest and the Slieve Bloom Mountains in south. The old Grand Canal connects the Shannon and the Barrow rivers and passes through Tullamore, the principal county town. The Tullamore name is well known because it was the original home of the distillery that made Tullamore Dew, one of the better brands of Irish Whiskey. West, along the Shannon, is one of the earliest Celtic monasteries and probably the most important one in the country, Clonmacnoise. Continuing south on the River Shannon brings you to Shannonbridge. This is the meeting point of the counties Offaly, Roscommon and Galway, and was once considered to be strategically important, hence the large artillery fortification dating from the Napoleonic era. A visit to County Offaly would not be complete without a visit to Birr with its famous Castle. Home of the Earls of Rosse, the Castle is also the home of the Rosse Telescope built in 1845 by the 3rd Earl and for three quarters of a century it remained the largest telescope in the World. It has been restored and is operational to this day.

The County Arms Hotel

BIRR

We were in Birr at a Jazz weekend when we discovered what a brilliant place it was for a break. Birr is the most complete Georgian Town in Ireland with uniquely fine squares, malls and streets of splendid houses. Overlooking this wonderful scenario is Birr Castle, world famous for its giant telescope, and home of the Earl and Countess of Rosse whose ancestors acquired the Castle in 1620. There is something for everyone in Birr, history, architecture, culture, and fun.

THE COUNTY ARMS HOTEL

The first time we stayed at the County Arms we stayed in a very pretty room with a bay window overlooking their wonderful historic walled gardens – it has stuck in my mind to this day. However, The Country Arms has been completely upgraded. The main house, which was built in 1809, has been restored to its original Georgian splendour and there has been an addition of 62 new bedrooms all designed to 4 star standard. There are suites, executive suites, deluxe family rooms, interconnecting rooms – everything you could possibly want. There is also a fabulous new Leisure Club – The Springs – with Wellness Suites for all the rejuvenation and pampering you will want on your stay. Elemis products are used at The Springs and whether you have an Aroma Spa Ocean Wrap or an Exotic Lime & Ginger Salt Glow you will have expert therapists looking after you. I am a great believer in

time for oneself – so send him to the Leisure Centre with the kids!

After all the beautifying and relaxing you will just be in form to visit their new Trilogy Brasserie Restaurant and terrace, which now overlooks the beautiful walled gardens. Having these wonderful gardens and greenhouses means you can be really sure that they are using local produce. Their Chef has travelled the world bringing back the benefit of his Australian and Asian experiences so the food will always be interesting. Locally sourced beef is just delicious, as is the slow roasted lamb shank – falling off the bone…and the confit of duck leg likewise. They have a superb wine list that I am sure even the good Earl would approve. They have special package rates available throughout the year so that you have no excuse for not combining genteel culture with good food, state of the art facilities, and health benefits.

Most importantly, The County Arms is still a family run hotel and the very professional Loughnane family know how to look after their guests.

Owners	The Loughnane Family
Address	Birr, Co. Offaly.
Tel	057 9120791
No of Rooms	70
Price	
Double/twin	€160
Single	€100
Family	€200
Suites	€520
Dinner	Yes - Restaurant
Open	All Year
Credit Cards	Yes
Directions	Approach Birr from either N52 or N62. Hotel is on edge of town on N62.
Email	info@countyarmshotel.com
Web	www.lucindaosullivan.com/countyarmshotel

Spa NET H P

County Roscommon

Sitting to write about County Roscommon brings back happy memories of many weeks spent boating on the River Shannon, which borders the county to the east. We would rent a cruiser in Jamestown and sail downriver under the bridge at Roosky past Tarmanbarry into beautiful Lough Ree and on down through Athlone et al. We did occasionally stop for a little drop of nourishment in some of the friendly pubs on the way. Roscommon town a pleasant place for a visit has the quaint story about its County Jail, now housing a collection of shops and restaurants. Apparently it was the scene of all the hangings in the county and used to have a woman executioner by the name of Lady Betty. She had her own sentence for murder revoked provided she did the job unremunerated. Strokestown is a well-planned town with an exceptionally wide main street, the idea of some former bigwig who wanted to boast the widest street in Europe. Strokestown

"Between two evils, I always pick the one I never tried before."
(MAE WEST)

Park House, designed by Richard Cassels, with its beautiful gardens and Famine Museum is well worth a visit. Heading west from Strokestown through Tulsk, the home of the legendary Queen Medb, who caused her share of trouble, you come upon Frenchpark, which gave the country its first President, Douglas Hyde, who was also one of the founders of the Gaelic League. Go south a little to Castlerea where it is worth stopping to visit Clonalis, which is the ancestral home of the O'Conor Clan, Kings of Connaught. Clonalis House has a number of interesting paintings charting the family's colourful history at home and abroad. To the north of the county is the town of Boyle on the banks of a river of the same name, an area that has become attractive to many artists, musicians and crafts people and warrants a visit to the Cistercian Boyle Abbey consecrated in 1220.

Gleeson's Townhouse & Restaurant

In the past few years people have come to appreciate the natural unspoiled beauty of Counties Roscommon and Leitrim, which have become destinations for the canny traveller wanting to find something different. Roscommon Town has plenty to do and see, including the enormous well-preserved Roscommon Castle built by the Normans in 1269, burnt down by the Irish four years later, and rebuilt in 1280. Right in the centre of the town is Gleeson's Townhouse & Restaurant, and this is where you are going to stay. Your hosts will be the very hospitable Eamonn and Mary Gleeson. Indeed, often Eamonn accompanies visitors to traditional Irish music "Sessiuns" held locally - and Mary is very involved in the Farmers Market which takes place on Fridays right beside their house – so she will show you the ropes there. That sort of hospitality and friendliness is what defines Gleeson's and which can be very hard to find in these Celtic Tiger Days. Both former school teachers, the Gleeson's bought the 19th century Manse (a Protestant Minister's House) in a derelict state in 1990, with the intention of opening a small café and B & B.

The comfortable accommodation offers a choice of standard or superior rooms, and one lovely suite overlooking the town's historic square. All rooms have free internet access, direct dial telephones, and satellite television and superior rooms have kingsize beds. Gleeson's is a member of Feile Bia, which demonstrates a commitment to using quality produce in their restaurant, The

Manse. Try the Toulouse sausage with bacon and creamy pasta or the crispy duck salad, followed maybe by the roast loin of local lamb, and do pick a decent bottle from the plentiful wine list. Actually, you will never go hungry in Gleeson's because they also have a very good Café which opens for breakfast from 8 a.m. doing delicious home cooked casual food and scrummy cakes and buns all day. Have a look too at the fine stonework and the historic archway at ground level opposite the turf fire stove.

By the way, if you are a golfer or an angler there is a centre for you with cold room, drying room storage and laundry facilities and, they are conveniently next door to a Leisure Centre. They also have a lovely self-catering apartment to let on the waterfront at nearby Lanesboro. The Gleesons seem to have thought of everything to make their guests happy.

Owners	Eamonn & Mary Gleeson,
Address	Market Square, Roscommon, Co. Roscommon.
Tel	0906 626954
No. Of Rooms	19
Price	
Double/Twin	€120
Single	€60
Family	€150 (2 adults + 2 Children)
Dinner	Yes – Restaurant and Cafe
Open	All Year – Closed 25th 26th December
Credit Cards	Visa MC Amex Diners Laser
Directions	Roscommon Town Centre; Next door to Tourist Office – County Museum.
Email:	info@gleesonstownhouse.com
Web:	www.lucindaosullivan.com/gleesonstownhouse

County Sligo

This is a county of scenic beauty and historical interested loaded with magical names like Coney Island, Dead Man's Point, and Inishfree, which is closely associated with famous Irish names such as W.B. Yeats, Countess Markiewicz, and Eva Gore Booth.

Sligo town is one of the busiest and fastest growing towns in the West and manages to be relaxed and busy at the same time. It boasts an Arts Festival in May, Summer Festival late July, Yeat's Summer School in August and Choral Festival in November.

Rosses Point, about five miles from Sligo town is an ideal spot for a day at the beach with a beautiful Atlantic view with the outline of Coney Island and its neighbour Oyster Island on the horizon. If your interest is in something more energetic, Strandhill's magnificent beach with its huge Atlantic breakers is a popular venue for surfers. At Strandhill you can try your hand and your body at the seaweed baths which are claimed to relieve stress, rheumatism and arthritis- and leave the skin beautiful too. Not very far away, are the ruins of Carrowmore Megalithic cemetary. This is said to be the largest such cemetary in Europe and possibly the oldest. On top of the nearby Knocknarea Mountain is Medb's Cairn which some say is the tomb of the legendary Queen Medb of Connacht whom they say was buried upright so she could keep an eye on the enemy!

Furtther west is the village of Aughris, home to an early monastic site, and a promontary fort. Continue west towards Easkey where two Martello Towers were defensive positions during the Napoleonic era. Easkey is also popular for surfing.

Just close to Sligo town is the lovely village of Ballintogher on the banks of Lough Gill, known as the Town of the Causeway. Further south is Ballisodare with the remains of a 7th century monastery. On to Collooney, or the nearby village of Riverstown, home of Sligo Folk Park. Further south the market town of Ballymote boasts the 14th C castle built by Richard de Burgo (Red Earl of Ulster). If you are into traditional music, Gurteen is a popular and thriving centre for it. For me probably the most peaceful and atmospheric place in the county is the small austere cemetary and church at Drumcliffe under the shadow of nearby Ben Bulben mountain where the poet W.B. Yeats and his wife are buried under a headstone inscribed "Cast a cold eye on life. On death. Horseman pass by."

"Writing free verse is like playing tennis with the net down."
(ROBERT FROST)

Kingsfort Country House

C'est si bon was the first impression of Kingsfort Country House in the little village of Ballintogher in County Sligo. And C'est si bon was the second impression too, for there are just some people who always get things effortlessly right. This place is chic, chic, chic without even trying. We have two destinations for our holidays each year – Ireland and France – we never change – but when we arrived at Kingsfort there was this distinct feeling that this was the perfect combination, a melange of the best of Irish and French for, at Kingsfort, Bernard and Corinne serve the most delicious French Irish food and wines.

Kingsfort Country House was originally a Courthouse built in the 18th C but it has been magnificently restored and decorated to provide much needed superb accommodation and hospitality for visitors to Sligo. There are ten bedrooms, all beautifully furnished in that understated rustic French style that we have all been trying to emulate from the magazines over the past few years. Six of these are in the courtyard of the main house. There is great flexability in the rooms available, two are interconnecting, which is ideal for families; most can be used as a twin or double, and there is also a room suitable for those with physical disabilities. Some open directly to the garden and some have a balcony. The garden is very pretty and there are sweet little French style garden tables where you can sit and sip on balmy days.

For cooler days there is a very warm comfortable sitting room with open fire and cable television. Each evening in the little diningroom, their chef prepares delicious dinner sourced on a day to day basis from a local organic farm and butchers. Two choices on each course are offered each night – it might be a colourful Mediterranean tomato pie with pesto and olive oil to start, or maybe an aubergine mousseline with pan-fried garlic mushrooms, followed maybe by Irish sirloin steak topped with butter or pink peppercorn sauce,or roasted seabass fillets and red pepper slices with Irish whiskey cream sauce – French style of course.

Whether you are on the Yeats trail, or playing on one of the six local golf courses, Kingsfort Country House is a really warm, friendly and atmospheric place to stay.

Pets are allowed too but not in bedrooms.

Owners	Bernard Eucher-Lahon and Corinne Ladonnis
Address	Ballintogher, Co .Sligo.
Tel	Tel: 071 9115111
No of Rooms	8
Price	
Double/twin	€130-€160
Single	€ 55- € 65
Family	€ 50 - €70 pps
Dinner	Yes – 24 hours notice required.
Open	All Year save 24 – 27 December
Credit Cards	Yes
Directions	Take Dromahair direction and then signs for Ballintogher. The house is in the village.
Email	info@kingsfortcountryhouse.com
Web	

www.lucindaosullivan.com/kingsfortcountryhouse

 NET P

County Tipperary

Tipperary is the largest of Ireland's inland counties. Situated in the rich fertile lands of the Golden Vale it is also a very wealthy county.

Without a doubt, the most outstanding of its many attractions is the Rock of Cashel, rising sharply to over 200 feet and topped by mediaeval walls and buildings. Not far from Cashel is the peaceful town of Cahir on the River Suir with its wonderful Castle dating back to the 13th and the 15th centuries, an Anglo Norman stronghold of the Butlers, the Earls of Ormond. North of Cashel the River Suir passes through the towns of Thurles, not far from Holy Cross Abbey, and is the birthplace of the G.A.A., the ruling body for our National Games. Templemore is like Westpoint on flat feet, being the training headquarters of the Irish Police Force, the Garda Siochana. The area around Nenagh and Lough Derg – Terryglass, Coolbaun, Puckaun -is very popular now with many people having holiday homes near the Lake. Nenagh also boasts a colossal round Castle Keep with walls 20 feet thick and a height of 100 feet topped with 19th century castellations. Clonmel is probably Tipperary's prettiest centre. It was the principal base for Bianconi, the most successful coach company in the 1800's in this country. Clonmel also boasts the 19th century St. Mary's Roman Catholic Church, the 19th century West Gate and the Greek Revival style Wesleyan Church and more. The county has many peaceful and pleasant villages to appeal to visitors such as Bansha, not far from Cahir and backed by the Glen of Aherlow and the Galtee Mountains, or Ballyporeen whose claim to fame is that U.S. President Ronald Regan's grandfather hailed from there.

"An actor's a guy who, if you ain't talking about him,
ain't listening"
(MARLON BRANDO)

Ashley Park House

The first time I saw Ashley Park House I took a deep intake of breath and thought I had entered the film set of Gone With the Wind or Raintree County. It is a most dramatic and unusual house for this part of the world which would do Savannah proud. An 18th Century house, a white vision with elaborate green painted verandahs, overlooking the sultry Lake Ourne, with hanging weeping trees. Ashley Park House is on 76 acres of beechwood and formal gardens, with strolling peacocks and ancient walled gardens, and is quite spellbinding. Friend Carmel and I had whirled up in my little blue MGF open topped car. Sean Mounsey, the family patriarch complete with cap, who is one of the greatest characters you are ever likely to meet said, "I want you to be happy here Ma'am". I felt like Princess Margaret. Sean took us up to the "Bishop's room" where he had put up a small temporary bed beside the half tester as the house was full and, looking puzzled, said half to himself, "I wasn't expecting two such fine strapping women as yourselves – now if one of you were smaller". Tears streamed down our faces we laughed so much, and as Carmel collapsed over the dressing table in a heap, Sean Mounsey beat a hasty retreat...

Ashley Park House has some of the finest rooms you will ever come across, and you can live out all of your Scarlett O'Hara fantasies in this house. The front bedrooms at either end of the house are vast, splendid and romantic. The house is magnificently furnished with impeccable taste by Sean's daughter Margaret. Relax in the impressive drawingroom with a drink in front of the fire or chill out in the beautiful octagonal Chinese reading room off it. Explore the old walled garden which they are restoring. Dine in the magnificent diningroom. Go to Ashley Park quickly you might not find Rhett

Butler but you will find Sean Mounsey, and his beautiful daughter Margaret, and they are much more interesting altogether. Children are welcome. It is incredible value and an equally incredible experience.

Owners	P.J. and Margaret Mounsey
Address	Ashley Park, Nenagh, Co. Tipperary.
Tel	067 38223
No. Of Rooms	5
Price	
Double/Twin	€110 - €120
Single	€55 - €60
Family	€110/€120 + (Children 50% over 2 years)
Dinner	Yes (Book by 2 p.m.)
Open	All Year
Credit Cards	Visa MC Diners Amex
Directions	From Nenagh, turn right on the N52 for 3 miles. Ashley Park is the large white house on the opposite side of lake.
Email	margaret@ashleypark.com
Web:	www.lucindaosullivan.com/ashleyparkhouse

Bailey's of Cashel

Bailey's Hotel is a mélange of the best of the old and the new. The original very fine old house, which fronts onto the main street of Cashel was built in 1703 by The Wesley Family, so is just over 300 years old, and has a great history.

Dermot and Phil Delaney are your very hospitable and friendly hosts here. They have transformed what was a very successful Guest House into a lovely family run hotel. Phil's impeccable taste is evident from the moment you set foot on the black and white tiled floor of the Hall of the main house, with its lovely historic Farrow & Ball colours. The bedrooms are beautifully furnished, both in the old house with its high ceilings, and the new. With Bailey's morphing into a hotel, there is now a fab new swimming pool and leisure centre. The addition of their cracking new contemporary restaurant No 42, doing really good modern food, has meant that even more so, Bailey's is now the focal point for Cashel's discerning diners. Their atmospheric Cellar Bar is where you will meet the locals, have a jar and enjoy the chat, and they also serve delicious casual bar food there. Being so well located in the town, you can just leave the car and walk

around and do the shops and sights, returning for a casual lunch or to the drawing room to relax. . Phil herself is a natural cook and a generous one to boot. She is the type of Chef who bakes two types of Bread for Sunday Lunch crusty white soda bread and a dark brown bread.

Bailey's is a superb place to stay when visiting Ireland's most famous monument, the famous Rock of Cashel. It is also a great spot for a short break – there are lots of golf clubs and pubs and places to see such as the Cashel folk village, Cahir Castle, the picture postcard Swiss Cottage at Cahir and much much more. Oh if you want a bit of ceoil and rince there are sesiuns in the Bru Boru Heritage Centre from June to September.

Owners	Dermot & Phil Delaney
Address	Main Street, Cashel, Co. Tipperary.
Tel	062 61937
No of Rooms	33
Price	
Double/twin	€150 - €180
Single	€95
Family	€190 - €220
Dinner	Yes – Restaurant and Bar Food
Open	All Year
Credit Cards	Yes
Directions	In Cashel Town

NET P

Email	info@baileys-ireland.com
Web	www.lucindaosullivan.com/baileyshotel

Bansha Castle

I got a tall order from an English PR agency representing the head of a large Legal Firm. "The Boss" was suffering Hip Hotel Fatigue and looking for something different. He wanted to rent a big Country House where he could entertain his best customers for a week. If it was that simple I would, as they say in Tipperary, be away on a hack, but no, he wanted more and a lot more. He wanted a house where he could self cater and indulge his passion for cooking some nights, and have dinner provided other nights. Still simple you may say but he also wanted a place where he and his friends could hunt, shoot and fish and be within walking distance of the local pub Well you will be delighted to know that I found the perfect retreat at the 18th C. Bansha Castle. As I travelled the road from Cashel to Bansha, it reminded me a little of Beverly Hills without the traffic for it definitely had the mansions, secure Stud Farms and prime beef units. This is 4-wheel drive territory so I knew when I arrived at Bansha Castle that I had backed a winner for Mr. Lawyer. Teresa and John Russell are welcoming hosts and there is a great casual welcoming feel to the whole house. You just know where you can throw your riding jacket on the hall stand, and leave your riding boots at the bottom of the stairs, without fear of reprimand.

Teresa will organize the Huntin', Shootin', Fishin' and she can also organize a beautician to come if you want to pamper yourself. The Drawing room is a impressive room with a large full size SnookerTable just off.

Perfect for someone with a wasted childhood in Pool Halls or for a visiting member of the Mafia. Teresa has organized the House so well that you can rent the whole place and have a private kitchen and dining room at your disposal or she will cook breakfast and dinner for you at times to suit you. If the house is not let then you will have the opportunity to stay on a B & B basis, and also be able to enjoy a dinner at one of her beautifully laid tables in the large Dining Room where she serves up good unpretentious home cooking. This arrangement also suits people celebrating special occasions, even divorces, and you can bring your own booze.

Owners	John & Teresa Russell
Address	Bansha, Co. Tipperary.
Tel	062 54187
No. Of Rooms	6 (for self catering sleeps 12/17)
Price	
Double/Twin	€100
Single	€65

The Castle is available for self-catering. It sleeps 12/17
Price on application.

Dinner	Yes – Has to be pre-booked.
Open	All Year
Credit Cards	None
Directions	Located just outside village of Bansha
Email:	johnrus@iol.ie
Web:	
www.lucindaosullivan.com/banshacastle	

 P

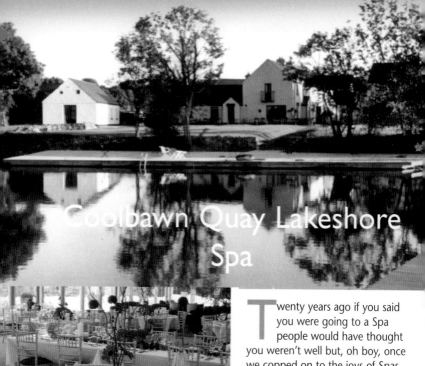

Coolbawn Quay Lakeshore Spa

Twenty years ago if you said you were going to a Spa people would have thought you weren't well but, oh boy, once we copped on to the joys of Spas did we ever take to them like ducks to the proverbial waters. Spas are for you, for me – not just a Leisure Centre where you are "working" watching the kids splash around, or a Health Farm where you go and pay for the joy of starving. Finally there is a place where we can go, be pampered, forget all our worries, have delicious healthy food and just crash out and rejuvenate.

Coolbawn Quay is a unique private village nestling on the shores of Lough Derg, complete with magnificent marina. Understated and elegant, accommodation is in a series of snug village rooms, larger lakeshore suites, or in luxury cottages with French doors to a private decking area. I watched a legendary movie star being interviewed on T.V. and he was asked what was the secret of his long marriage - "separate bathrooms", he replied. At Coolbawn Quay they obviously realise this so, their luxurious cottages have a choice of 2, 3 or 4 bathrooms. Here you will receive full hotel style service and, indeed, you may also dine in your cottage. Alternatively, cottages can also be taken on a self-catering basis.

The Aqua Spa Suite comprises a counter-current pool, sauna and steam room, as well as a relaxation room overlooking the lake. There are all sorts of body wrap treatments, Algimud Body Masks; Deep Sea Black Mud envelopment and facials using the holistic Dr. Hauschka and Rene Guinot products. I had the Algae Seaweed Body wrap which was fabulous leaving my skin exfoliated and feeling like silk. Facials for men are superb too, designed to rejuvenate tired skin.

Owners Jay and Kevin Brophy are also in to food, they once owned a top Dublin restaurant, so you are going to enjoy the very best of delicious fare, using fresh local and organic produce, beautifully prepared by their Chef and served in a the candlelit diningroom. Oh there is a bar too, where you can also imbibe and/or have lunch. Coolbawn is on my agenda for regular de-stress visits.

Get the girls together, you deserve it, or take Himself – maybe he deserves it too – it's the sort of Lough Derg you can both really enjoy!

Owners	Jay & Kevin Brophy
Address	Coolbawn, Lough Derg, Co. Tipperary.
Tel	067 28158
No. Of Rooms	48
Price	
Double/Twin	€190 - €230
Single	€125 - €145
Family	As Above + Children 3-12 years receive 33 %
	Discount pps sharing rates (€95-€115pps)
Dinner	Yes – Restaurant
Open	January to December (Closed Christmas)
Credit Cards	Visa MC Amex Diners Laser
Directions	From Nenagh N52 to Borrisokane for approx
	1Mile, turn left opp AIBP factory, on to Lake
	Drive Route. Pass through villages of Puckane
	and Coolbawn Entrance exactly 2 miles past Coolbawn Village on left.
Email	info@coolbawnquay.com
Web	www.lucindaosullivan.com/coolbawnquay

NET Spa H P

Inch House

Eamonn de Valera was President when I was a child. A very old man at that stage, he was almost blind and was an austere and forbidding figure sitting up in the back of the old State Car wearing a black hat. To me he was a terrifying sight and I didn't like him at all. Well, whatever I thought about the man, he got his own back because when I got married I was in a fairly pressurised job and when we moved into our new house the timing of the move, arranged three months in advance, was down to seconds. The carpet layers were coming first along with the plumbers. De Valera upped and died and the Nation went into mourning. His funeral was on the day of the move, the carpet layers went out in sympathy, whilst the furniture removers from the old house didn't, hence the furniture arrived first and the carpet layers arrived after dark much the worse for the wear …

INCH HOUSE
John and Nora Egan's Inch House in Thurles sits proud in the middle of lush farmland with a drive up to the stately front door. The first thing you notice about Inch, is the meticulous care given to the pot plants outside the door – perfectly cared for but the second thing I noticed was the portrait of Dev over my bedroom door! Get John Egan talking about politics and you could have the fun of your life – he is gregarious and brilliant all in one. Nora laughs quietly in the background at the good of it all while she overseas this meticulous well cared for house. Have a

drink in the beautiful William Morris papered blue, white and gilt, drawingroom and listen to the local stories. The Restaurant attracts people from all over the place for the ample well prepared food served by wonderful ladies who will look after you like a mother. The House was the former home of the Ryan family for hundreds of years– a great Tipperary name- and in fact shortly after I wrote about Inch House I had an email from the Ryans in New Zealand where they have now made there home. Have a look at the stained glass Ryan coat of arms on the staircase the family motto was "Death Before Dishonour". The bedrooms are peaceful and comfortable and you will recline on the finest linen in a Prince Albert bed before coming down to a lavish breakfast in the magnificent diningroom again. It is a beautiful house on wonderful grounds and I can't wait to get back there again.

Owners	John & Nora Egan
Address	Thurles, Co. Tipperary.
Tel	0504 51348
No. Of Rooms	5
Price	
Double/Twin	€116
Single	€68
Dinner	Yes - Restaurant
Open	All Year
Credit Cards	Visa MC Laser
Directions	From Thurles take Nenagh road for 6 kms past The Ragg. House is on the left.
Email	mairin@inchhouse.ie
Web:	www.lucindaosullivan.com/inchhouse

County Waterford

A walled city of Viking origin, Waterford is the oldest city in Ireland and even today it retains much of its medieval character. It is the home of Waterford Crystal, the world-famous handcrafted, cut glass product. The parameters of the 10th century settlement can be clearly identified in The Viking Triangle. Reginald's Tower is the most historic urban medieval monument in Ireland while the elegant Chamber of Commerce building, the City Hall and the Bishop's Palace are prime examples of beautiful 18th century architecture. Waterford has a long theatrical and musical tradition, which centres on the historic Theatre Royal, which hosts the Waterford International Festival of Light Opera each year. East of the city is the pretty village of Passage East with its ferry service to Ballyhack in Co. Wexford. Stay on the coast road south to the long sandy beach, flanked by woodland, at Woodstown ideal for a quiet stroll or gentle dip in the sea. Go further south to the popular holiday village of Dunmore East which is largely undiscovered by tourists, or go west to the honky tonk family holiday town of Tramore. Further west is the busy commercial town of Dungarvan but swing inland to the beautiful hidden stretch of the River Blackwater around Cappoquin within three miles of Lismore and its ecclesiastical past and most dramatic castle in the country, Lismore Castle, owned by the Duchess of Devonshire. It is a fabulous area and also largely undiscovered by tourists. If you want to learn a few words of the native tongue drive back south to the Irish speaking area of Ring where the language thrives as do other traditions such as music and set dancing.

"Never drink black coffee at lunch, it will keep you awake all afternoon"
(JILLY COOPER attrib)

Athenaeum House Hotel

"I watched the Tall Ships sail gracefully by from here – it was absolute heaven", I said to friend Miranda. We were sipping champagne on the terrace of Zak's Restaurant at the Athenaeum, a chic new boutique hotel on ten acres, with views down over the river Suir and marina at Waterford Harbour. The best of modern classical taste and design has gone into the Athenaeum – not a frill in sight - just clean lines and stunning colours. From the Grand Piano in the elegant anti-room to the beautiful side chairs in the hall, the Athenaeum is different. Cardinal purple carpets lead down to the bedrooms, which are understated and elegant, but with funky chairs, flat screen television, modem connections, fridge, and anything else today's discerning traveller might want.

Stan Power and his wife Mailo own the Athenaeum and they cannot do enough for you. Stan is so cool, professional and helpful, I would imagine if he had been captaining the Titanic it would have made it to New York. Mailo is an Interior Decorator and is responsible for the slick beautiful cool décor with its clean architectural lines and modern classical atmosphere, which has been wowing the who's who of Irish society, who have been beating a path to their door.

Zak's Restaurant, which is one of the most attractive dining rooms in the country, runs across the back of the hotel. Long and conservatory style, with those great views, you won't however be too distracted from what is on your plate, which is just delicious and also very well priced. Do have dinner and think Tartare of diced salmon, onion, capers and chives, wrapped in a saffron cream and salmon pearls, or lightly sautéed foie gras on brioche served with duck liver pate with caramelised apple chutney followed, maybe,

by the pinkest rack of lamb with aubergine Provencal or Dover Sole. You can look forward to a lovely breakfast too – try their muesli complete with cardamom seeds – they could sell that by the stone weight and make a fortune.

This lovely boutique Hotel on the banks of the River Suir is a real find.

Owners	Stan & Mailo Power
Address	Christendom, Waterford City, Co. Waterford.
Tel	051 833999
No. of Rooms	29
Price	
Double/Twin	€130
Single	€100
Dinner	Yes – Restaurant
Open	All Year
Credit Cards	Visa MC Amex Laser
Directions	From roundabout at Railway Station take N25 in direction of Wexford. After traffic lights take first right on to Abbey Road, then first right after hump back bridge.
Email:	info@athenaeumhousehotel.com
Web:	www.lucindaosullivan.com/athenaeum

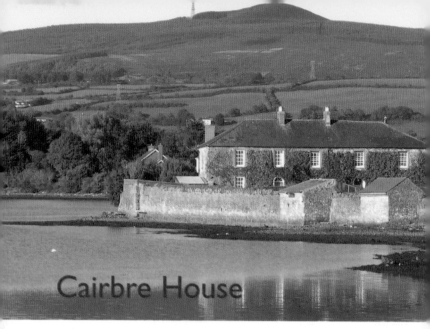

Cairbre House

As you drive out of Dungarvan towards Dublin, you will see on the estuary to the left, a beautiful ivy clad Georgian house sitting virtually on the water. I had looked at this house and wondered for years what it was all about. One day I took the bull by the horns, turned off the main road, and drove up for a closer look. Stepping gingerly through the gates I suddenly found I was in a world that reminded me of Jane Austen, for behind the big boundary walls was a very beautiful olde world garden of roses and herbaceous borders. It just seemed like heaven and, to cap it all, who strode around the corner but Mr Wickham! Brian Wickham, quite unfazed by this nosey person at his door, welcomed me warmly and took me through his lovely home, which has been in his family for over 100 years.

Cairbre House was built by the Duke of Devonshire in 1819 and it is sitting on the Colligan River Estuary sheltered and protected with a backdrop of Cruchan and the Comeragh Mountains. It is quite stunning, understated, and a gardener's paradise. The walls surrounding the property were built at the same time as the house. Made of limestone they give protection to the amazing gardens, which enjoy a microclimate, allowing a large number of rare and unusual Mediterranean, South African, Australian and other sub tropical plants to be grown successfully.

The house has beautiful features. There is a very comfortable drawing room for guests use with a blazing fire. The bedrooms are comfortable and pretty and it is amazing to wake up in this lovely historic

atmosphere – but with all modern comforts! Brian's breakfasts are super. You can have the traditional Irish Breakfast but at Cairbre it will be with free range eggs and potato bread plus herbs from the garden, or kick the morning off with succulent local Helvick smoked salmon on brown bread with scrambled egg and a garden salad decorated with fresh herbs and flowers. He also does a lovely hot vegetarian special with tomatoes, courgettes, mushrooms, peppers and chives sautéed in a light olive oil with fresh herbs, topping it off with edam cheese and grilling it for a few minutes – and you can have Earl Grey tea if you ask nicely. Jane Austen would approve of Mr. Wickham.

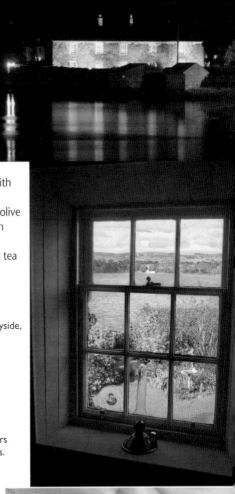

Owner	Brian Wickham
Address	Strandside North, Abbeyside, Dungarvan, Co. Waterford.
Tel	058 42338
No of Rooms	4
Price	
Double/twin	€76-€86
Single	€42-€50
Family	€38-€43pps + 50% reduction children under 12. If under 3 years free sharing with parents.
Dinner	No
Open	Mid Feb – Mid Nov
Credit Cards	Yes
Directions	From Waterford approaching Dungarvan remain on N25. Take right hand exit off 2nd roundabout
Email	cairbrehouse@eircom.net
Web	www.lucindaosullivan.com/cairbrehouse

Foxmount Country House

Our French visitors, Michelle and Zandra, had expressed a definite interest in visiting the Waterford Glass Factory so, the decision was taken, to drive down and overnight in Waterford. We drove down through Wicklow, the Garden of Ireland, and Wexford and duly did the tour of the Waterford Glass Factory. Living in Paris, the idea of an Irish farm appealed and I had one up my sleeve. They took a sharp intake of breath when the ivy clad Foxmount House came into view. "Oh, this beautiful", they exclaimed of its impeccably kept lawns, glorious flower beds and gravel paths, that looked as if they had been fine combed. Inside, too, they were delighted with a blazing fire in the drawingroom, as they admired the family silver, antiques, and general good taste of Margaret and David Kent who, with their son and daughter, run this lovely house and dairy farm to perfection. Michelle and Zandra were anxious to explore the farm so David took them under his wing and showed them around. Some time later I looked out my lovely bedroom window and was surprised to see the pair of them belting a ball back and forth out on the tennis court, but what struck me most when I gazed out the window was being able to see into Margaret Kent's kitchen where perched on the windowsill was a perfectly arranged bowl of soft and dewy pink roses. For me, that said it all. Foxmount House is perfection, from the sign on the main road, right through to the hidden sections of the kitchen. Breakfast was beautifully presented with little bowls of floating flowers and leaves. Delicious breads and scones with homemade preserves sit on beautiful plates followed by a delicious cooked breakfast. I couldn't resist picking up all of the plates and looking underneath to see who made them! One of the brilliant things about Foxmount too is its location. It is a farm on the edge of Waterford City so you are in to the centre by taxi or car in literally ten minutes, yet you have the joy of being close to the sea, you are on the road down to the little ferry in picturesque Passage East and very close to any number of golf courses

Owners	David & Margaret Kent
Address	Passage East Road, Waterford.
Tel	051 874308
No. Of Rooms	5
Price	
Double/Twin	€110
Family	€55pps
Single	€70
Dinner	No
Open	Mid March – 1st November
Credit Cards	No
Directions	Take Dunmore East Road from Waterford City, then take Passage East Road for one mile. Sign on right for house.
Email	info@foxmountcountryhouse.com
Web	www.lucindaosullivan.com/foxmount

213

Glasha Farmhouse

You know that great Irish welcome that we all boast about and very often don't find – well you can be sure of it at Olive and Paddy O'Gorman's lovely Glasha Farmhouse set in the beautiful Nire Valley. It is a large white house impeccably maintained and, as you drive in and get out of your car with your bags and baggage, you are suddenly swept up in the enthusiastic warm welcome that Olive bestows on everyone – no wonder she was the first B & B to win the Failte Ireland Warm Welcome Award. Before you know where you are, you are ensconced on comfortable sofas being plied with tea and apple tart while Olive talks a dime a dozen. Paddy is delightful, a gentle smiling farmer, who knows and is proud of what Olive has achieved and her enthusiasm for visitors and tourists. Olive has thought of everything for the very comfortable bedrooms, with all sorts of extras like electric blankets, hairdryers and nick nacks often lacking in good hotels – and some rooms have Jacuzzi baths. The Nire Valley is very popular with walkers and anglers but you can drive around like me if you wish!! These are the real hidden places of Ireland very often not found by Tourists as they beat a track for the West. The river Nire runs beside Glasha and fishing permits are available locally. Have a delicious dinner – maybe Rack of Comeragh Lamb or Poached Monkfish and, if you are good, Olive and Paddy will show you the back gate, which slips out onto a little windy road where at the foot of the hill is one of the dinkiest old pubs I have ever been in. It is like something out of a movie – absolutely wonderful and a perfect way to end the day before strolling back up to Glasha for a wonderfully peaceful sleep in the stillness of Ballymacarbry. Come down next morning and you are in for one of the

best breakfasts in Ireland – what a spread Olive puts out – you will have the camera out – it is one of the best I have ever seen. Houses like Glasha are the real hidden places of Ireland very often not found by the tourist. You are in for a treat.

Owners	Paddy & Olive O'Gorman
Address	Glasha, Ballymacarbry, via Clonmel, Co. Waterford.
Tel	052 36108
No. Of Rooms	8
Price	
Double/Twin	€100
Single	€60
Family	€120
Dinner	Yes
Open	All Year except Christmas
Credit Cards	Visa MC
Directions	Signposted on Clonmel to Dungarvan Road
Email	glasha@eircom.net
Web	www.lucindaosullivan.com/glasha

Richmond Country House

Richmond House is the real thing – no faux Georgian facades here - everything about it is real, classy, elegant and understated. The house, built in 1704 by the Earl of Cork and Burlington, looms tall and stately, gazing serenely out over the fields and private parkland, in the heart of the Blackwater Valley. It has been the Deevy family home for forty years or so as Jean Deevy and her late husband raised their six children there. To aid the restoration and upkeep of such a large house, Jean started out simply doing Bed & Breakfast when en-suites were "en heard of". She provided very well cooked homely food, introducing to her repertoire the "rage of the time" the old prawn cocktail – always being a winner. Times move on and Richmond House is now a place to be reckoned with for Jean's son, Paul, is a very fine Chef, having trained in the Hotel Industry, moving on then to Switzerland, before returning to take up the reins at Richmond House along with his wife, Claire. The bedrooms are gracious and spacious, furnished with antiques, and so comfortable you just want to snuggle in there and not move out. Have a drink in the old conservatory or in the butter yellow drawingroom, meet the people, who will be salivating at the thought of Paul Deevy's innovative but classically French oriented food. Think Fresh Chorizo risotto with steamed mussels and a light butter sauce followed by local fillet

of lamb with tapenade, sundried tomatoes and a rosemary jus … have the Crinnaugtaun apple juice at breakfast…it helps the hangover.

Richmond House is a perfect place to stay for visiting West Waterford including the beautiful Lismore Castle, which is literally just down the road. The whole area is absolutely beautiful with lots of interesting inhabitants and places to visit, and you will be at the heart of it in Richmond House.

Owners	Paul & Claire Deevy
Address	Cappoquin, Co. Waterford.
Tel	058 54278
No. Of Rooms	9
Price	
Double/Twin	€150
Single	€75
Family	€160
Dinner	Yes - Restaurant
Open	January 23rd – December 23rd
Credit Cards	All Major Cards
Directions	Take Waterford Road from Cappoquin, Richmond House is on the right.
Email	info@richmondhouse.net
Web	www.lucindaosullivan.com/richmond

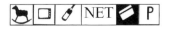

Waterford Castle Hotel & Golf Club

S omebody said to me one time "Waterford Castle is decorated just the way a Castle should be". Rich and regal with lavish antiques, ornate plaster ceilings, and all the elegance of the original features preserved, it is just perfect. From the moment you pass through the carved granite arch and the studded oak door into the amazing hall, dominated by a beautiful Elizabethan stone cavernous fireplace and magnificent tapestries from generations of yore, you are in another world. You will notice on the chimneybreast, raised proud from the stone like some giant ornate jewel, the carved Fitzgerald coat of arms. Likewise the crested carpet on the floor, for Waterford Castle, built in the 15th Century, and the Norman Keep before that, was in the hands of the Fitzgerald family for 800 years. Fabulously located on its own private 310 acre island estate on the River Suir, yet just 2 miles out of the hustle and bustle of Waterford City, the Castle is surrounded by woodlands and an 18 hole Championship Golf Course. How do we get to the island, I can hear you ask? You just nip out the Dunmore East Road, turn left at the sign and head down to the private ferry which transports you across the little channel into another world of luxurious retreat, sanctuary and seclusion. Over a thousand years ago the first inhabitants cut a rough track to their secure settlement but this is now a tree lined driveway, lush, with ever changing colours and ahead stands the stunning Castle, picturesque and enchanting.

The splendid guest rooms and suites are bright and airy with magnificent

views of the surrounding estate and golf course. Guests get the feeling, for this is the way that they are received, that they are residents rather than "hotel guests". Dinner in the Munster Dining Room with its original oak panelled walls and ornate ceilings is a memorable occasion. The Chef will tempt you with perhaps Kebabs of Dublin Bay Prawns with Roast Garlic, Basil and Cherry tomatoes followed by such delicious goodies as Moroccan Spiced Fillet of Aged Beef with cous cous salad and a Pepper Salsa Verde. Go and be a part of this Fairy Tale lifestyle.

Owners	Gillian Butler (General Manager)
Address	The Island, Ballinakill, Waterford.
Tel	051 878203
No. Of Rooms	19
Price	
Double/Twin	€235 - €420
Single	€180 - €265
Family	€415 - €605
Dinner	Yes - Restaurant
Open	Open All Year save 24th 25th 26th Dec and 3rd Jan – 5th Feb.
Credit Cards	All Major Cards
Directions	Look out for sign to left off Dunmore East Road.
Email:	info@waterfordcastle.com
Web:	www.lucindaosullivan.com/waterfordcastle

18h | NET | H | P

County Westmeath

A county rich in fertile farmland and an important producer of beef with a wide area for dairy farming. Mullingar, the central town, is no sleepy town but a busy commercial trading centre with its own traffic congestion problems. One of the town's claim to fame is that in 1951 it hosted a music festival which became an annual celebration of traditional music, An Fleadh Ceoil, which now moves about the country to a different town each year.

Westmeath has many attractions including its lakes in the northern part of the county around Castlepollard and well worth visiting. Close to Castlepollard is Lough Derravaragh, which is famous for the legend of the Children of Lir. Lir, King of Connacht, whose second wife, jealous of Lir's love for the children of his first wife, turned them into swans condemned to remain so for 900 years. Many people visit this area for its fishing – mainly roach, pike and trout.

If something a bit stronger than water is needed, a trip to Kilbeggan and Lock's Distillery Museum, could fill the bill. The entrance fee includes a free sample which certainly enhances the tour. In the west of the county is Athlone town, the traditional centre of Ireland. Situated where east meets west, and north meets south, on the River Shannon, it is an ideal spot from which to visit the islands and shores of Lough Ree to the north and historical ruins at Clonmacnoise to the south.

"A farm is an irregular patch of nettles, bounded by short term notes, containing a fool and his wife who didn't know enough to stay in the city."

(S.J. Perelman)

Shamrock Lodge
Country House Hotel

Athlone is a busy bustling lively place spanning the mighty River Shannon. It is a halfway house for the pleasure boats that negotiate the river from north of Carrick-on-Shannon to Limerick in the south. It is also an ideal central place from which to tour and investigate the many places of interest in midland Ireland. Steeped in history, the town walls were built by the Normans in 1257. Part of these walls are still in evidence and the 13th C Castle stands proud on the west bank of the River Shannon. Another great attraction is the nearby medieval site of Clonmacnoise founded in 548AD. As a monastic city, it flourished under the patronage of the kings, including the last High King of Ireland, Rory O'Connor, whose remains were buried there. (1198AD). Athlone boasts numerous excellent recreational facilites, not least being Athlone Golf Club at Hodson Bay , a short distance outside the town, which must be one of the finest inland courses in the country.

To enjoy a visit to any town depends on finding somewhere pleasant, comfortable and enjoyable, to stay and the Shamrock Lodge Country House Hotel has all the necessities to provide these pleasures. The Hotel was beautifully refurbished in 1991 with all modern luxuries while still retaining the Country House atmosphere. A new additional development was opened in 2005 which transformed the Shamrock Lodge of yore into a hip cool destination.

From the moment you enter the elegant reception area, you feel the friendly and luxurious ambience. Go to your room and enjoy the comfort and ease that only beautiful décor and facilities can provide. Visit the fab Iona Bar, overlooking the gardens where friendly and courteous service and good

drink will put even the most depressed into good humour. Their An Luain restaurant produces excellent cuisine sourcing only fresh and local produce – so you can expect to enjoy the best of Irish Angus beef fillet maybe on a bed of pepper relish or delicious panfried seabass with tomato caper and olive salsa but whatever is on the menu you can be sure you wont be hungry.

The Shamrock Lodge is also ideal for small parties, or large parties, or even a romantic tryst for just two – you can bring pooch too but check first.

If the standard of an hotel is the people who stay there then a list of former guests includes Princess Grace, Queen Salote of Tonga and President Mary Robinson.

Owners	Paddy McCaul
Address	Clonown Road, Athlone, Co. Westmeath.
Tel	09064 92601
No of Rooms	52
Price	
Double/twin	€150
Suite	€295
Dinner	Yes - Restaurant
Open	All year save Christmas 24th – 26th inc
Credit Cards	Yes
Directions	From Town Centre - go over the Town Bridge and veer left around by Athlone Castle. Follow one-way system to Battery roundabout (Walsh's pub on left). Drive straight and take immediate turn left after Battery Bridge. Hotel entrance further on, on the right.
Email	info@shamrocklodgehotel.ie
Web	
www.lucindaosullivan.com/shamrocklodgehotel	

County Wexford

The Vikings have a lot to answer for when you think of the number of Irish Towns they have founded. Wexford in the southeast, the sunniest part of the Country, is another example of their handiwork. It's very narrow streets are now teeming with thriving shops and businesses and, along the quayside, on the Slaney estuary stands a statue to Commadore John Barry, the Wexford man who founded the U.S. Navy during their War of Independence. This lively town is host to the ever popular and important Wexford Opera Festival every year. South of the town, almost on the extreme southeast corner of the country is Rosslare Strand with its magnificent beach and two 18 hole golf courses. Rosslare Strand is very popular with Irish people but very often missed by tourists who disembark from the ferry at Rosslare Harbour and drive madly out of the area. Going north the county has many towns with historic connections and none more so than Enniscorthy. Enjoy its period atmosphere and its connection with the 1798 Rebellion with its backdrop of Vinegar Hill site of a famous battle of the same name. Also worth seeing is the Pugin designed St. Aidan's Cathedral. Of more recent interest are the sandy beaches at Curracloe where Steven Speilberg shot those realistic battle scenes for his movie "Saving Private Ryan". In the south west of the county, on the banks of the Barrow Estuary in the quaint village of Arthurstown close to Dunbrody Abbey and less than a mile from Ballyhack from whence the ferry runs to Passage East in County Waterford.

ARTHURSTOWN
IS NOT A TOILET
Please _STOP_ your dog
using it as one

225

Aldridge Lodge

A great attraction of France are the little restaurants with rooms where you will dine on superb rustic food at reasonable prices and not have to worry about driving afterwards.

Well, I found a real little gem in Ireland called Aldridge Lodge in Duncannon, Co. Wexford. Duncannon is right down on the coast, a world apart, and definitely worth a detour. Driving past Aldridge Lodge you would just think it was any modern dormer style brick house, but behind this "Wisteria Lane" suburban façade is an ultra modern restaurant with a few simple but charming bedrooms upstairs for guests. Seriously talented Chef Billy Whitty, whose father is a local fisherman, met his partner, Dublin girl, Joanne Harding, whilst working in another Country House. They are a lovely pair and have created this smashing restaurant, on two levels, with cool white walls, modern paintings and girls in long black bistro aprons in attendance.

This is seriously good food, beautifully cooked and presented, at bargain basement prices. Dinner is €35 and if you want to indulge in lobster it will cost you maybe a fiver or a tenner more – can you believe it? Even at those prices we were brought an amuse bouche of brown crabmeat and little Mediterranean vegetables – olives, peppers and breadsticks. We kicked off with panfried fillet of John Dory with buttered asparagus and a brace of succulent seared Kilmore Quay scallops served in an intense pool of Hook Head Lobster bisque, perfectly judged and quite sublime. We followed up respectively with pan fried fillet of hake with chorizo sausage, scallop, and a pepper orange and lemon butter, and a baked whole lobster on an enormous white plate topped with a fluff of deep fried noodles

As for puds – try the Tasting Plate for Two which had beautiful little morsels of sticky toffee pudding, warm apple puff pasty lattice, Wexford strawberries, Peach Schnapps parfait, chocolate hazelnut caramel torte with chocolate fudge sauce.... get the drift!

We weren't feeling any pain when we fell upstairs to bed!! By the way they do a cracking Sunday lunch too. Children and pets are welcome by prior arrangement.

You should be salivating and rearing to go – if not there is something wrong with you!

Owners	Billy Whitty and Joanne Harding
Address	Aldridge Lodge, Duncannon, Co. Wexford.
Tel:	051 389116
No of Rooms	3
Price	
Double/twin	€100/110
Single	€50
Dinner	Yes – Restaurant
Open	February- December
Credit Cards	Yes
Directions	From Duncannon village follow directions for the Hook Lighthouse. House located 1 km on this road on the left.

Email
info@aldridgelodge.com
Web
www.lucindaosullivan.com/aldridgelodge

Glendine Country House

ARTHURSTOWN AND BALLYHACK

From whichever side you approach Arthurstown and Ballyhack on the Hook peninsula, there is a positive feel of never neverland. Coming from either Dublin or from Rosslare, the Duncannon roundabout outside Wexford is where you change worlds. Sit back and head straight out towards Ballyhack, trundling through hedgerows, along miles of straight road downward towards the sea, taking you little by little back into history to this totally undeveloped area. From the Waterford side, you take the car ferry at Passage East,it only takes a few minutes but the scene is set and as you approach Ballyhack and its 16th Century Castle you are almost exhilarated. Have a pint of the black stuff in the local pub you deserve it after that five minute voyage!

GLENDINE COUNTRY HOUSE.

Tom and Ann Crosbie's fine Georgian Country House sits on 50 acres of beautifully landscaped gardens and paddocks, which hold their Highland cows, Jacob sheep (the ones with the curly horns) and deer. A Dower house to the Dunbrody Estate it was first occupied by the Chichester family and later by land agents until one of them absconded with the Nursery Nurse causing a great scandal. Glendine retains many of its original 1830 features, and, overlooking the Barrow Estuary, all of the rooms are stylishly beautiful and all have magnificent sea views. Beautifully decorated, using soft historic Farrow & Ball colours, the original large en suite bedrooms have Victorian beds, pitch pine floors, crisp cotton sheets, original wooden shutters. In the past year a wing of new bedrooms has been added and these too are absolutely beautiful, large and spacious. All rooms have T.V. and all mod cons. The lovely yellow drawingroom with fine fireplace, antiques and works of art, is comfortable and welcoming. Breakfasts are hearty and wholesome, where possible using organic produce.

Help yourself to a fine range of fresh fruits, cereals, porridge, yoghurts and juices followed by delicious cooked breakfast with lashings of wholemeal toast or homemade brown bread. Two cosy 4****Self catering cottages are available in the courtyard, converted from the original 1830 stone buildings, and these sleep five people comfortably. Dinner is not available but soup and open brown bread sandwiches are happily provided at all times. There are very nice Restaurants close by and excellent pub grub. Glendine has a wine licence but you can bring your own. This is a gorgeous house, Tosh and Annie are charming hosts, and you couldn't find a finer place to stay.

Owners	Tom & Ann Crosbie
Address	Arthurstown, Co. Wexford
Tel	051 389500
No. Of Rooms	6
Price	
Suite	€120 - €140
Double/Twin	€110 - €120
Single	€60 (supp €20 July + August)
Family	€140 (2 Ad + 1 Ch) €160 (2 Ad + 2 Ch)
Dinner	No (Light Suppers Only)
Open	All Year except Christmas
Credit Cards	Visa MC Diners
Directions	From New Ross turn right at Brandon House Hotel Pass JFK Arboretum, Arthurstown is signposted.
Email	glendinehouse@eircom.net
Web	www.lucindaosullivan.com/glendine

     NET P

Kelly's Resort Hotel & Sea Spa

ince 1895 four successive generations of the Kelly family have each added their own stamp to Kelly's Resort Hotel. Bill Kelly and his wife, Isabelle, have, in turn, enlarged and added a whole new cool modern dimension in the last few years culminating in the addition of the fabulous new SeaSpa incorporating eleven treatment rooms, seawater vitality pool, rainforest shower, rock sauna, lanconium, steam room, mud chamber and seaweed bath, which has been their biggest project ever.

Being right on the beach there is that upmarket sandy resort ethos and atmosphere, for, as soon as you swish up and park, you will see people strolling around in bathrobes between Spa, Leisure, Beauty Centre, Hairdresser or Hot Tub – it is just switch off time. I know people who drive down to Kelly's, park their car, and don't move it again until they are leaving Rosslare Strand. Why would they, everything one could possibly want is encompassed within the Hotel. When one mentions Kelly's Hotel, people generally say – "Oh, the food is fabulous, and one eats so much". That's true. It's like a cruise ship, non-stop wonderful food all included in your rate.

Breakfast and lunch are available buffet style in the Ivy Room or with formal service in the gorgeous Beaches Restaurant, which had over a €1m spent on it alone not so long ago. Likewise with lunch, not forgetting afternoon tea and all day availability of free coffee. In the evening people gather for drinks before dinner - which is always superb - oysters, foie gras terrine, game, fish, just as much of anything you could want and Kelly's import their wine direct from France, where Isabelle's family are in the wine business in the Chateauneuf-du-Pape region, resulting in excellent very well priced wines. Dancing follows dinner so join in the fun. Bedrooms are lovely – some with doors opening out onto your own mini terrace or else have

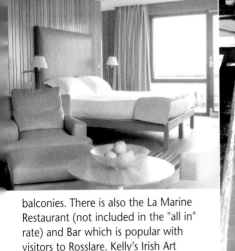

balconies. There is also the La Marine Restaurant (not included in the "all in" rate) and Bar which is popular with visitors to Rosslare. Kelly's Irish Art Collection is famed and in this regard it is opportune to mention that throughout the year there are different breaks revolving around Art, Cookery, Wine, Antiques, Gardening, Ballroom Dancing and of course golf. Kelly's mainly operates on an all-inclusive package, anything from two days to a week and, for what is included, it is superb value. Sometimes, midweek only, they do a room and breakfast rate if that is what you want and you can dine in either Beaches or La Marine. I don't think it is possible for Bill & Isabelle to carry out any further improvements!

Owner	Bill Kelly
Address	Rosslare Strand, Co. Wexford.
Tel	053 32114
No. Of Rooms	118
Price	
Double/Twin	€170 + 10% Service Charge
Single	€ 90 + 10% Service Charge
Family	On request
	Spring and Autumn inclusive rates from €280pps + 10% (for 2 days upwards)
Dinner	Yes – 2 Restaurants
Open	16th February to 9th December
Credit Cards	Visa MC Amex
Directions	On Rosslare Strand
Email	kellyhot@iol.ie
Web	www.lucindaosullivan.com/kellyshotel

Whites
of
Wexford

We got married in St. Mullin's in South Carlow and spent our first night in White's Hotel. The funniest part of the whole event was that the Bridesmaid got a double bed, the Best Man got a double bed, the other couple with us got a double bed, but even though a bottle of champagne had been sent to the Bridal Couple's room we got two single beds and we were too embarrassed to ask for a double!! That is all a very long time ago, needless to say, but White's Hotel is still a part of pivotal life in Wexford, but it is not the White's of yesteryear for it has been completely reconstructed. We went back for a look at the metamorphosis and were absolutely wowed by it all.

The new hotel now features a fabulous Tranquility Spa & Wellness Centre with a hydropool and thermal suite – that is apart from the Leisure Centre with 20m pool. In addition, they also have the first Cryotherapy Clinic in Ireland. It can be used for all sorts of medical conditions. So you won't have to go to Switzerland or America you can have a fabulous break combined and try the latest therapy.

The bedrooms are superb, furnished to 4 Star standard, big beds, crisp sleek and modern, plasma screen televisions, Broadband, minibar, iron and ironing board, in room safes, in house movie and satellite channels. They also have a very large number of family rooms – so bring the kids folks – they will love it.

Being a food critic, I suppose I tend to always come back around to the restaurant and bar facilities and at Whites of Wexford they are superb. There are two bars, the Lobby Bar or the fashionable La Speranza Café Bar – you can have food throughout the day in both places. Their main Restaurant overlooks the Courtyard – where you can also sit out and enjoy a glass or ten of champagne or dine alfresco. Think along the lines of having crisp crab and prawn spring rolls with sesame noodles, baby bok choy, avocado puree and lime vinaigrette followed maybe by grilled fillet of brill with braised fennel, spicy chorizo, crushed potatoes and sauce vierge or maybe roast loin of venison with a smoked cheese and caramelized onion rosti, root vegetable puree and a light juniper and port reduction.

The boys of Wexford are being well looked after at Whites.

Owners	Peter Wilson (General Manager)
Address	Abbey Street, Wexford.
Te	053 91 22311
No of Rooms	157
Price	
Double/twin	From €118
Family	From €118 + €25 BB per child.
Dinner	Yes – Restaurant and Bars
Open	All Year
Credit Cards	Yes
Directions	In centre of Wexford.
Email	info@whitesofwexford.ie
Web	www.lucindaosullivan.com/whitesofwexford

Spa NET P

Houses in alphabetical order

Slow down

njoying Ireland is not about tearing down a motorway at 90 miles an hour, for doing it that way you will miss the whole ethos of the country. Tourists planning their trip in advance from America and other distant places tend to look at our little green, bear shaped, island in the Atlantic on the edge of Europe and think "we'll see it all in 3 days" – believe me you won't have even "done" West Cork properly in that time. You may have seen the views but you won't have experienced anything except a sore backside from sitting in the driving seat!

Take time out, get to know your hosts, it makes such a difference. They can give you all the local lore and recommendations. Go down to the local pub – you won't be long on your own – because the Irish love to talk. Every time I arrive at a destination, my first stop is the nearest hairdressers, which absolutely delights Brendan, for he then has an hour to find the best pub and in no time at all, the locals will have found out his seed, breed and generation, and he will have been rewarded with the best local information.

In the immortal words of Simon and Garfunkel - "Slow Down You Move to Fast..."

Unless otherwise stated room prices include breakfast. Apart from Hotels we suggest that you make arrangements for dinner on the night of your arrival at the same time as you book your accommodation as most houses would like 24 hours notice.